Being Present

A Book of Daily Reflections

David Kundtz

Conari Press

This edition first published in 2015 by Conari Press, an imprint of
Red Wheel/Weiser, LLC
With offices at:
665 Third Street, Suite 400
San Francisco, CA 94107
www.redwheelweiser.com

ISBN: 978-1-57324-644-6

Library of Congress Cataloging-in-Publication Data available upon
request.

Cover design by Jim Warner
Cover photograph © Andy Roberts/Getty
Interior by Maureen Forys, Happenstance Type-O-Rama
Typeset in Monotype Garamond Pro and Proxima Nova

Printed in Canada.
MAR
10 9 8 7 6 5 4 3 2 1

Contents

Acknowledgments

Many thanks to Robert Stenberg and Brendan Collins, who read the text and made valuable and appreciated comments.

Thanks and special appreciation to Jan Johnson and Rachel Leach, publisher and editor, and all at Conari Press for their support and help in preparing the text.

Introduction

We shall not cease from exploration
And the end of all our exploring
Will be to arrive where we started
And know the place for the first time.

T.S. ELIOT

The goal of this little work is clear: to encourage and facilitate your capacity to be more mindful and awake to the present, and thus achieve the peace that comes only from living in the moment, being present in the "now," as you live the cycles in a year of life. This is a work about increasing your ability to attend, to pay attention—being mindful, being present.

Some Considerations on Mindfulness

As I consider what to say about mindfulness, I experience a challenge: to express in words what is so utterly simple, neither a magic quick fix nor a miracle cure, but rather a deep well of possibilities worth a lifetime of exploration. Also, I like the phrases "being aware" and "being awake" because they are more commonly understood and, unlike what often befalls "mindfulness," avoid the categories of buzzword and cliché. Here are a few descriptive statements, culled from my own experience as well as the masters.' Mindfulness is

- Paying full attention to what is going on right now by staying in the present moment

- A balanced observation of what *is,* without criticism or judgment

- Noticing the changes happening in and around you

- An awake and aware participation in life

We all have experienced mindfulness, but chances are those experiences are fairly infrequent because of the constant state of distraction in which we live. Some examples:

Mindfulness is the moment when you're out walking and suddenly see a deer, before you react, when it's just you and the deer—no thinking, no fear, no judging. It's an uncontaminated moment of attention. You are mindful.

Another example, from Thich Nhat Hanh, the Vietnamese Buddhist monk, who spoke so eloquently about washing dishes: When you are washing the dishes, simply wash the dishes, noticing the warm soapy water, the hardness of the plate, the act of cleaning . . . That's all. Attend to what you are doing. Mindful.

There is the moment of mindfulness when you look into the eyes of the woman behind the counter as she gives you change and you smile and say thank you. At that moment you are present to her, acknowledging a relationship, even if it's fleeting; your attention, your appreciation is on her. In that moment you are mindful.

Mindfulness is noticing the subtle change in your spouse's demeanor this morning as you look across the breakfast table, and not just continuing to eat your cereal or read the paper—*not* noticing, or worse, *pretending* not to notice.

Mindfulness: *Being aware of and paying attention to the present moment as much as possible, non-judgmentally, in order to notice changes and be awake to its true meaning.* Mindfulness prevents us from missing life, from reaching life's end with the sad realization that the deepest human experiences have passed us by. *Now* is all we have; the past is gone, the future is not yet. Just now.

Suggestions for Use

The 365 reflections in this book are based on the cycles of life: the big one, from youth to old age; the four seasons and twelve months of the year; and the many other phases of daily life, such as work, family, health, and so forth.

We'll open in the age of youth, in the season of spring, and in the month of March—a time of new life and beginnings. We continue with young adulthood and summer, middle age and autumn, and old age and winter. Each month focuses on specific aspects of life, which are named at the beginning of the chapter. I suggest that you begin with the meditation for today's date and continue through the year.

Of course, use the reflections in any way that works for you—they are designed for those who are experienced in meditation as well as beginners. Each daily meditation is meant to be experienced as a two-part process. The first part consists of a quote and my brief comments. It is focused on thoughts, feelings, mind wandering, and ideas. The second and longer part is the mindfulness phase, the part that you create. This is an open awareness, a "calm abiding," a receptive process of becoming still. Each meditation is designed so that the first part brings you into the present moment with some quiet consideration and so leads you to the second part. I suggest the following:

> Read the quote and comments slowly, perhaps twice. Then quietly consider what you've read. Think about it for a moment or two. Any feelings? Agree or not? Hang out with the idea, let your mind wander with it a bit. This first part should help you become quiet and focused and still; it can be brief.

c swirl ↶ at the end of the
your sign of invitation into
dfulness part, the part you
our time *right then and there,* in
he thoughts and feelings go, let the
de into silence, let your mind
iet and simply observe your
ul quietude. Be still. Turn
your breathing. Breathe
me back to your breath.
, try to be as still as you can,
nd with no specific expec-
e process. What happens

end each day may vary—a
ore, maybe less. As you
elop your own patterns
and rhythms of briefly reading/considering and then qui-
etly meditating. Any time of day will do, but consistency
will help your process.

The emphasis is not on the quote and few lines of
commentary. Though carefully chosen, they are not the
point. The point is what you bring to the moment, what
happens for you after you've read them and let them go.
What they lead you into then and there is the point; how you bring

that mindful awareness into all the ups and downs of your life is the point. That *feeling* and *sense* of being mindful—right now for a few moments and throughout all the cycles of your life—is the point. In your meditation you are growing and developing a habit of mindfulness; in all the moments of your life, you are applying and exploring your habit.

As you proceed, keep these points in mind:

Getting it right: Please don't make meditation complicated! I repeat, *above all*, don't ask yourself, "Am I doing this right?" You are. I can't emphasize that enough. Consider that thought, if it comes, as a distraction (see below). The process is simply turning your attention within, without judging yourself or anyone else, and noticing what is happening or what isn't. It's doing nothing; utterly simple, often challenging.

The "rules" are not hard and fast, really—as you get into the process, experiment as you like. This is a key idea and once you've got it, you've gained a great advantage.

Trust: Similarly, trust what happens for you as you practice, even if it feels messy and unstructured. Then, trust the power of being still and in the present moment to bring you a new level of awareness, if for no other reason—and there are many—than because all the world's spiritual traditions have affirmed it for centuries.

Distractions: When (not "if") distractions come ("Did I turn off the oven?" "Did I lock the door?" "Am I prepared for the meeting?"), simply notice them and promptly release them, in one swift motion, in one door and out the other, rather than engaging with them or fighting them. Then simply return to focus on your breathing.

Please note that part of the process of mindfulness meditation is dealing with distractions; it's part of the territory. The mind is always busy, and this busyness takes many forms: worries, agitations, feelings, thoughts, desires, sleepiness, doubts, and so on. An entire meditation time spent in dealing with distractions—noticing-them-come-letting-them-go and returning to focus on your breathing—is a successful meditation.

Breathing: This is basic to your meditation: always come back to your breathing. If distractions continue or if you find you need to "do" something, always come back to your breathing, simply noticing the breath in and the breath out. Turn your mental focus inward—in whatever way you interpret that.

Your body: In meditation, your body is not your enemy; it has its gifts and its needs, so keep your mindfulness "embodied," lest it become too "heady" or disengaged from the earthly body. Imagine yourself as mindbody. Most people find that sitting in a comfortable yet alert position is best. Avoid positions that might induce you to sleep. If you find yourself physically uncomfortable, jumpy, or nervous, try pacing—walk slowly back and forth in a small space or confined circle, and be mindful of each step. In this practice your coming-back-to-focus technique can be your breathing and/or each deliberate step.

Mindfulness and Exploration

One of the hazards, as well as benefits, of contemporary life is abundance. There is so much of everything—which leads to complexity, which by nature begets forgetting. Then, often tragically, you forget that you forgot, and thus an important insight is permanently lost. If nothing else, your daily mindfulness meditation helps you to not forget what you don't want to forget.

If you're like me, you'll find that the most challenging part of being mindful is the non-judging part. It's one thing to be non-judgmental if an experience is agreeable, but it's another when some idiot in a huge vehicle forces you off the road into a ditch. You see what I just did? "Some idiot." The fact is, I don't know anything about him. Was he distracted because he just lost his job or had some other difficult experience? Is he not an idiot at all? It comes back to me, to what I bring to my moment. I know nothing about *his* moment.

Experienced meditators speak of having the beginner's mind rather than the mind of an expert. While the latter knows the answers, the former is not so sure, and is open to learn new answers, new experiences. Cultivate a beginner's mind.

I ask you to consider yet again: Do not fret about your meditation practice, whether you're getting it right or not. It's right. Even if you never get to the second part of the meditation, the mindfulness part, don't worry or judge yourself. "Mind wandering" and just "spacing out" are psychologically beneficial. Your meditation is not so much about what happens for you as it is about how you respond to whatever happens.

Keep in mind that this practice of mindfulness is a twofold journey, a double blessing: first, the mindful time *right now* as you consider new ideas and let go into a quiet period of stillness; second, that very stillness that will expand into all the moments of your life, transforming them into moments of deeper awareness and compassion, into ongoing mindfulness. If the first does not lead to an enrichment of the second, it's not accomplishing all it is meant to accomplish.

So, later in the day or week, whether you're in a stressful situation or simply going about day-to-day living, you will have the awareness, the equanimity—the mindfulness—that you need and want in order to "be present."

You will have become a more mindful person, you will notice what you want and need to notice, you will do what you want to do, you will be who you want to be. Listen to an experienced voice:

> *Spiritual practice is not just sitting and meditating. Practice is looking, thinking, touching, drinking, eating, and talking. Every act, every breath, and every step can be practice and can help us to become more ourselves.*
>
> THICH NHAT HANH

The opening epigraph to this introduction offers the much-quoted lines from the poet T. S. Eliot's "Four Quartets." It seems an appropriate theme for our exploration of mindfulness and being present; after all, seeking to become more mindful is a true exploration—perhaps the most worthy one of all—for it is an exploration into yourself. My hope is that as you explore your life cycles, you will often know many places—again and "for the first time."

Part 1

Spring and Youth

March

Nature and Beauty

March 1

Spring is nature's way of saying, "let's party!"

ROBIN WILLIAMS

It's the season of new life and new hope.

No matter what has gone before.

Now is the time to have a party—whatever that might look like for you.

Just be sure to have some fun.

March 2

Some monarch butterflies—they're beautiful with the black and deep orange wings—fly up to 2,500 miles to get out of the cold weather and hibernate.

That's a long way to go to keep warm.

Imagine a butterfly traveling 2,500 miles.

This amazing planet holds so many mysteries . . .

March 3

If people did not love one another, I really don't see what use there would be in having any spring.

VICTOR HUGO, *Les Miserables*

So spring, says Victor Hugo, is for encouraging people to love one another?

What is there about the relationship between spring and the human being that makes a young person's fancy turn to thoughts of love?

Springtime—love—you. Put them all together.

March 4

Some people walk in the rain; others just get wet.

ROGER MILLER

It all depends on your attitude.

In your mind's eye, imagine yourself out in the rain.

How do you want to *be* in that rainy moment? Rehearse it now.

Live it when the rain comes.

March 5

What a strange thing!
to be alive
beneath cherry blossoms.

KOBAYASHI ISSA

Why is it strange?

What picture do Issa's words form in your mind?

Look at that picture for a moment.

Then let it fade . . .

Close your eyes . . .

March 6

The love of the body of man or woman balks account, the body itself balks account,

That of the male is perfect, and that of the female is perfect.

WALT WHITMAN, *"I Sing the Body Electric"*

Bring your awareness to your perfect body—overlooking for now the possibly various ways it is not perfect—and see the beauty!

The beauty!

March 7

*Youth is, after all, just a moment, but it is the moment, **the** spark, that you always carry in your heart.*

RAISA GORBACHYOVA

Some believe and teach that the person you are at ten years old—your likes, dislikes, beliefs, assumptions, and so on—is the person that you become for life. Thus, the values and events of the world during the year you were ten will give you insight into yourself.

What was going on in the world the year you were ten?

Is that you?

March 8

The landscape belongs to the person who looks at it . . .

RALPH WALDO EMERSON

So much,
of so much value and beauty,
of so much grandeur and excellence,
   . . . is free.

Picture your favorite freebies.

March 9

Look deep into nature and you will understand everything better.

ALBERT EINSTEIN

The words "deep into nature" imply time spent looking.

What "nature" would you like to look at more deeply?

Then, just go and look.

March 10

From the poet e. e. cummings:

sweet spring is your

time is my time is our

time for springtime is lovetime

and viva sweet love

There's that theme again.

Ah, well, why fight it?

How does "viva sweet love" fit into your life?

March 11

We have to get back to the beauty of just being alive in this present moment.

MARY MCDONNELL

So, really, there's a creative statement of the theme of this whole book.

Mary McDonnell is a successful film, stage, and television actress. Those are fields from which one does not necessarily expect an insight into mindfulness, right? Indeed, the stereotypical understanding of celebrity life is of the fast-moving, what's-next, and I-don't-have-time variety, right?

What a nice surprise.

Do you too have surprises?

March 12

The best remedy for those who are afraid, lonely, or unhappy is to go outside, somewhere where they can be quite alone with the heavens, nature, and God.

ANNE FRANK

I have been aware of this quote from Anne Frank for many years. Yet, every time I read it, I am amazed and full of awe. How could a girl of twelve or thirteen, living in fear and hiding from the Nazis for two years, have the insight, grace, and maturity to make such a confident and wise statement (among many others)?

She—and so many others we know nothing of—is a testament to the nobility of the human spirit at any age.

One feels gratitude. What else?

March 13

If you do something that you're proud of, that someone else
understands, that is a thing of beauty that wasn't there
before—you can't beat that.

TELLER

Recall a moment when you were proud of something you
did, said, were part of . . .

"That is a thing of beauty . . . that wasn't there before."
But it is now and always will be.

No, you can't beat that.

March 14

Forget not that the earth delights to feel your bare feet
And the winds long to play with your hair.

KHALIL GIBRAN

Perhaps the earth's delight comes from the fact that you
are both of the same stuff and it recognizes you.

Your dancing feet . . .

Your hair blown by its wind.

March 15

Beware the Ides of March . . .

. . . are the words Shakespeare put in the mouth of the soothsayer, warning Julius Caesar of his impending death.

The middle of March is as good a time as any to contemplate death. The more at peace you can become with your own death, the more you will be a peaceful and mindful person in life.

But now, simply notice your life-giving breath—in and out . . .

March 16

Beauty is truth, truth beauty—that is all
Ye know on earth, and all ye need to know.

JOHN KEATS, *"Ode on a Grecian Urn"*

It seems to me the only way to understand this is in utter simplicity—to look for no nuanced distinctions, no philosophical insights.

"What you see is what you get and it's all beautiful?"

Or maybe not . . .

March 17

Sure and you've got to keep your own spirits up, for there's no one else will do that for you!

JACLYN MORIARTY

Keeping your spirits up means keeping your mind in the moment.

(So much of suffering is the anticipation of it.)

So sometime, dance an Irish jig.

Then, just be still.

March 18

The poet and naturalist Edward Abbey offers these words: *There is beauty, heartbreaking beauty, everywhere.*

"Heartbreaking beauty." What's that? Can beauty break your heart?

And it's everywhere . . . this beauty.

Do we need to watch out?

March 19

Sylvia Plath, often a dark poet, gives us these joyful words:

I felt my lungs inflate with the onrush of scenery—air, mountains, trees, people. I thought, "This is what it is to be happy."

This seems to describe a moment of insight, of happiness . . . which can often happen in an unexpected moment, like the inhaling of a breath (and air, mountains, trees, and people).

March 20

In the spring, at the end of the day, you should smell like dirt.

MARGARET ATWOOD

Gardening is a wonderful way to be in the moment.

To be grounded.

Of the earth.

Can you imagine a way to get involved with the dirt of the earth?

Imagine it.

March 21

There are about as many molecules in a thimbleful of water as there are thimblefuls of water in all the oceans of the Earth.

CHET RAYMO

Do you—as I—have a difficult time wrapping your mind around that?

Nevertheless it's true.

So much beyond our imagining! So much!

Imagine . . .

March 22

I can calculate the number of thimblefuls of water in the sea, but I have no way of knowing how many galaxies there are in the universe . . . or even how many universes might exist.

CHET RAYMO

Maybe read that again. Then:

. . . from contemplating universes

to placing yourself in this moment right now . . .

In this little dot of a place, here . . .

It can help with perspective.

March 23

Una de las cosas más agradables de la vida: ver cómo se filtra el sol entre las hojas.

One of the most pleasurable things of life: to see how the sun filters through the leaves.

MARIO BENEDETTI

Ah simplicity!

I recall once when sun filtered through leaves gave me peace.

Can you?—or some similar natural event?

Watch for sun through leaves this spring.

March 24

Adopt the pace of nature: her secret is patience.

RALPH WALDO EMERSON

It might help in heeding this Emersonian advice to recall that we are indeed part of nature—so the leap to patience feels a bit closer.

Pace: the rate of speed one goes through life.

Yours?

March 25

This is from Mark Twain:

It's spring fever.

That is what the name of it is.

And when you've got it, you want—oh, you don't quite know what it is you do want, but it just fairly makes your heart ache, you want it so!

So many comments about spring deal with this theme: the longing of our hearts. For a moment, just be with *that feeling . . .*

. . . or recall it. After all, it is spring.

"You want it so!"

March 26

It is amazing how complete is the delusion that beauty is goodness.

LEO TOLSTOY

Think of instances when the beautiful is not good . . .

· . . . and the good is not beautiful.

Then bring to mind a happy moment when they do come together.

March 27

Sunshine is delicious, rain is refreshing, wind braces us up, snow is exhilarating; there is really no such thing as bad weather, only different kinds of good weather.

JOHN RUSKIN

Well, I can think of times when it would be hard not to call the weather bad:

Katrina, Sandy?

This brings to mind an old Swedish saying: There is no such thing as bad weather, just bad clothing.

So what's the weather right now? Good? Bad? Can you dress for it?

March 28

Early youth is a baffling time.

BRUCE CATTON

When you were young, do you remember thinking "How am I going to figure all this out?!"

So, how did you?

Or did you?

Or are you, like me, still figuring it out?

March 29

Sculptors, poets, painters, musicians—they're the traditional purveyors of Beauty. But it can as easily be created by a gardener, a farmer, a plumber, a careworker.

CHARLES DE LINT

Oh yes! Oh yes!

Has Canadian novelist de Lint hit upon an idea for our times?

Where is beauty for you?

Who creates beauty in your life?

In whose life are you the creator of beauty?

March 30

Pablo Picasso said:

It takes a long time to become young.

And Mae West added:

You're never too old to become younger.

Is youth mostly a state of mind—you're only as old as you feel?

I think the answer to that is yes and no.

Your yeses and noes?

March 31

Youth is happy because it has the capacity to see beauty. Anyone who keeps the ability to see beauty never grows old.

FRANZ KAFKA

So there's old and there's "old." How do you make the distinction?

Still want to see beauty?

Of course you do!

Goodbye, March, and on to April.

April

Relationships and Sex

April 1

Here cometh April again, and as far as I can see the world hath more fools in it than ever.

CHARLES LAMB

Fools. Suffer them gladly? Avoid them as much as possible? Occasionally join them?

In any event, please, let's not lose the grace to laugh at ourselves.

April 2

This is from Walt Whitman's "To You."

Let us two walk together aside from the rest;

Now we are together privately . . .

Come! Tell me the whole story,

Tell me what you would not tell your brother, wife, husband, or physician.

Intimacy.

It brings you into the here and now, perhaps like nothing else.

There are many ways to create intimacy, like sharing a secret.

Think of other ways.

April 3

Life is partly what we make it, and partly what it is made by the friends we choose.

TENNESSEE WILLIAMS

Ah, friends! In so many ways they make us who we are.

And of course, we in some way make them who they are.

Such responsibilities.

Such opportunities.

April 4

We are all born sexual creatures, thank God, but it's a pity so many people despise and crush this natural gift.

MARILYN MONROE

What most strikes me about these words is the source—a national sex symbol.

But of course, after the "despising" and the "crushing" she was, in the end, just Norma Jean, like you and me.

So, no despising, no crushing, please.

April 5

The weather here is windy, balmy, sometimes wet. Desert springtime, with flowers popping up all over the place, trees leafing out, streams gushing down from the mountains. Great time of year for hiking, camping, exploring, sleeping under the new moon and the old stars. At dawn and at evening we hear the coyotes howling with excitement—mating season.

EDWARD ABBEY

These simple, descriptive words from a devoted desert advocate and writer show both observation and appreciation, and between the words, love.

He loved the land, especially the desert Southwest.

Do you love some piece of land?

April 6

Le cœur a ses raisons que la raison ne connaît point.

The heart has its reasons that reason knows nothing of.

BLAISE PASCAL

This is perhaps one of the most quoted sayings in the Western world.

Why, do you suppose?

Because it's true? Yes, yes, of course.

But what else?

April 7

Youth is a silly, vapid state,
Old age with fears and ills is rife;
This simple boon I beg of Fate:
A thousand years of Middle Life.

CAROLYN WELLS

Well, maybe not a thousand—but a few more years in the middle would be nice.

You've been around the block a few times, and can still walk briskly.

April 8

The sexual embrace can only be compared with music and with prayer.

MARCUS AURELIUS

Of course, it's been compared to a lot more than that.

Can you choose a comparison—a simile or metaphor—for "the sexual embrace"?

Think on it a bit and see what you come up with.

April 9

When someone loves you, the way they say your name is different. You know that your name is safe in their mouth.

JESS C. SCOTT

It's really a beautiful thing to say:

"My name is safe in your mouth."

The words are built on such intimacy and trust.

Be blessed if they can be yours—or can be said of your mouth.

April 10

April hath put a spirit of youth in everything.

WILLIAM SHAKESPEARE, "Sonnet 98"

Here's the whole first stanza from Shakespeare's sonnet:

From you have I been absent in the spring,

When proud-pied April, dressed in all his trim,

Hath put a spirit of youth in everything,

That heavy Saturn laughed and leaped with him.

Seek that spirit in this April, "proud-pied in all his trim!"

April 11

Everything in the world is about sex except sex. Sex is about power.

OSCAR WILDE

Everything in the world, Oscar? Or are you perhaps given to embellishment and hyperbole?

But then we expect that from you—and a lot of things *are indeed* about sex, right? Like what?

But maybe don't spend too much time on that question . . .

April 12

The meeting of two personalities is like the contact of two chemical substances: if there is any reaction, both are transformed.

CARL JUNG

Who has transformed you?

And thus, have you transformed?

Makes for interesting reverie.

April 13

I am well aware that for some, love and passion do not always follow the traditional path.

AMANDA QUICK

People are who they are.

Your approval and encouragement

or my disapproval and condemnation

change nothing,

but can add to conflict and pain

or to harmony and peace.

April 14

"Why is it," he said, one time, at the subway entrance, "I feel I've known you so many years?"

"Because I like you," she said, "and I don't want anything from you."

RAY BRADBURY, Fahrenheit 451

"I like you."

What a strong, clear statement!

Combine it with "I don't want anything from you."

Sounds like a good formula for friendship.

April 15

The wages of sin are death, but by the time taxes are taken out, it's just sort of a tired feeling.

PAULA POUNDSTONE

Ah, taxes.

What controversies!

What bitter complaints!

What anger!

You and taxes: what's the relationship?

April 16

Love me when I least deserve it, because that's when I really need it.

SWEDISH PROVERB

Whether or not we have expressed this sentiment, I'll bet we've all felt it sometime in our life.

Indeed, is love something that is deserved, or just there? Does it happen on its own and then be given freely, often without understanding why or wherefore?

Ah, love . . .

April 17

Indifference and neglect often do much more damage than outright dislike.

J. K. ROWLING

At least with an enemy who attacks, there is engagement, acknowledgment, no matter how negative. But with indifference, the soul withers; with neglect, life stagnates and dies.

It can be devastating.

April 18

Boys and girls in America have such a sad time together; sophistication demands that they submit to sex immediately without proper preliminary talk. Not courting talk—real straight talk about souls, for life is holy and every moment is precious.

JACK KEROUAC, *On the Road*

From the writer of the Beat Generation come some thoughtful words.

Can you do anything to reduce "a sad time" for boys and girls?

Have you an opportunity to talk to them with "real straight talk about souls"?

April 19

Anyone who stops learning is old, whether at twenty or eighty. Anyone who keeps learning stays young. The greatest thing in life is to keep your mind young.

HENRY FORD

Keep the synapses firing.

Keep the little gray cells alive.

How will (or do) you do that?

April 20

Real love amounts to withholding the truth, even when you're offered the perfect opportunity to hurt someone's feelings.

DAVID SEDARIS

I think he's talking about the practice of restraint—of not doing something that seems logical or expected or easy to do, because it's mean.

It takes a combination of self-confidence and kindness to do that, or better, to *not* do that.

Next time: Just don't do it.

April 21

My friends tell me I have an intimacy problem. But they don't really know me.

GARRY SHANDLING

There's nothing quite like self-blindness, is there?

Of course, on some deep level we know what's what.

This is a moment to have an honest friend.

April 22

The way you make love is the way God will be with you.

RUMI

For believers and non-believers alike, that's a provocative statement.

How does it strike you?

You reap what you sow? Is that the same thing in other words?

Which, when you think about it, is not always true, right?

Now let the thoughts go . . .

April 23

Most of us remember adolescence as a kind of double negative: no longer allowed to be children, we are not yet capable of being adults.

JULIAN BARNES

Child one minute, adult the next. It can drive parents crazy.

Until, if they are fortunate and insightful, they remember that it's normal and necessary.

Keep them as safe as possible, minimize damage, and wait it out!

April 24

Our wounds are often the openings into the best and most beautiful part of us.

DAVID RICHO

Know how I have suffered and you will have the key to my heart.

Lucky me if you use the key with care.

April 25

The poet Robert Frost offers these words from "Two Tramps in Mud Time":

The sun was warm but the wind was chill.

You know how it is with an April day.

When the sun is out and the wind is still,

You're one month on in the middle of May.

"Fickle" is what Frost seems to be saying about the spring weather.

Or is it about never being satisfied with what we have right now, always looking to the *past* or *future* for something better?

April 26

Equanimity: evenness of mind especially under stress.

MERRIAM-WEBSTER'S DICTIONARY

What an excellent word!

What a fine virtue!

What a rare trait!

What a treat when you see it!

April 27

We are not the same persons this year as last; nor are those we love. It is a happy chance if we, changing, continue to love a changed person.

W. SOMERSET MAUGHAM

. . . and a "happy chance" well worth pursuing. Keeping up with your changes, with mine, with ours—never mind the world's and everyone else's—we really are fortunate to maintain our love, now inevitably changed . . .

. . . but onward, always "we, changing, continue to love . . ."

April 28

Too many adults wish to "protect" teenagers when they should be stimulating them to read of life as it is lived.

MARGARET A. EDWARDS

No doubt about it: Adults are often scared of teenagers. Why? It must be because we remember, at least to a degree, what we were like—especially what we got away with—and we don't know what to do about it.

Lucky the teen with parents and mentors who are adults and unafraid.

April 29

Rose: *Do you love him, Loretta?*

Loretta Castorini: *Aw, Ma, I love him awful.*

Rose: *Oh, God, that's too bad.*

MOONSTRUCK

Earlier in the film, Rose says, "When you love them they drive you crazy because they know they can!"

Well, it's true, isn't it? When you love someone, you give them power to hurt you—and to heal you.

And to . . .

April 30

April showers bring May flowers.

TRADITIONAL SAYING

Sometimes. Sometimes not.

Depends a lot on weather conditions at the time and where you are on the earth. Snowing in some places; crocuses and daffodils in others; in others, the tropical sun beats down.

It's all relative.

May

Art and Spirituality

May 1

Today, depending on your circumstances, you can celebrate:

The season of spring with a maypole

The Virgin Mary, Queen of May

International Workers' Day

The Pagan festival of Beltane

Robin Hood and his merry men

A bank holiday

The Roman feast of Floralia

Lei Day in Hawaii

. . . and probably several others.

Find your reason and celebrate it however you want.

But celebrate something, someone, some moment . . .

May 2

As a painter I shall never signify anything of importance. I feel it absolutely.

VINCENT VAN GOGH

Van Gogh had no way of knowing that his paintings, which now sell for millions of dollars, would someday hang in the great museums of the world.

"I shall never signify anything of importance," he wrote, probably to his brother.

But he kept on painting what he saw . . .

May 3

Seek the sacred within the ordinary.

Seek the remarkable within the commonplace.

REBBE NACHMAN OF BRESLOV

How often we miss things!—insights, kindnesses, brilliance, wisdom, generosity, courage, and more. Why? Isn't it often because, to our quick observation, it seems "ordinary" and "commonplace?"

We don't expect it, so we don't notice it.

Seeking is often simply noticing.

May 4

Art is I, science is we.

CLAUDE BERNARD

The great French nineteenth-century physiologist emphasizes that art springs from the heart and soul of the person . . .

While science always needs corroboration.

Each following a different path to truth.

May 5

The world's favorite season is the spring.
All things seem possible in May.

EDWIN WAY TEALE

The winter has passed; the long, dark days give way to light and warmth.

We're ready to take on whatever comes.

What will you take on?

May 6

In order to be utterly happy, the only thing necessary is to
refrain from comparing this moment with other moments in the
past, which I often did not fully enjoy because I was comparing
them with other moments of the future.

ANDRÉ GIDE

This statement from Gide, the French writer, gives clear voice to the frustration that rises from a lack of mindfulness.

Judging from his writings, we can suppose that this insight brought him a deeper ability to be mindful.

May 7

I think it's a bit silly to brand the Internet as the "downfall of youth."

ERNEST CLINE

Every age brings its adult critics of the younger generation and its imminent downfall.

The Internet certainly has brought many things to the world—but I doubt very much if it's the downfall of youth.

What has it brought to you?

May 8

If you are truly aware of five minutes a day, then you are doing pretty well. We are beset by both the future and the past, and there is no reality apart from the here and now.

PETER MATTHIESSEN

Writer (*The Snow Leopard, Far Tortuga, At Play in the Fields of the Lord*), adventurer, and Zen priest, Matthiessen lived a full life.

" . . . no reality apart from the here and now . . . "

For the next few minutes—here and now, stillness and quiet.

May 9

Art is the symbol of the two noblest efforts: to construct and to refrain from destruction.

SIMONE WEIL

The "to construct" part is fairly obvious. But what do you suppose she means when she says that art is the symbol of refraining from destruction?

Hmmm . . .

May 10

Every year, back comes spring, with nasty little birds yapping their fool heads off and the ground all mucked up with plants.

DOROTHY PARKER

Lest we allow spring to be all sunshine and roses, Dorothy Parker, with her wit and wisecracks, gives us a dose of reality: mud, cold rain, and early birds interrupting your sleep . . .

. . . helping us to keep the balance.

May 11

It is only with the heart that one can see rightly;
What is essential is invisible to the eye.

ANTOINE DE SAINT-EXUPÉRY

I hope you've had the joy of reading *The Little Prince,* the source of the above quote (and one of the best-selling books ever published.) If so, you know what Saint-Exupéry is talking about here . . .

. . . and even if you have not read it, you still know what he's talking about, don't you?

May 12

Nothing is less real than realism . . . It is only by selection, by elimination, by emphasis that we get to the real meaning of things.

GEORGIA O'KEEFFE

She's talking, of course, about abstraction.

What in your life needs abstraction—some elimination, or some emphasis—for clarity?

May 13

We live in a society that is overscheduled, overcommitted, over-extended—and we like it that way!

If a moment opens up in our lives it does not present a peaceful opportunity for reflection or awareness but rather a space to be filled.

BROTHER TOBY MCCARROLL

The worrisome words here are "and we like it that way!"

Perhaps acknowledging that you actually like many aspects of a fast-paced life is the first step in achieving what you might really desire: slowing down a bit.

Consider for a moment.

May 14

Art is in love with luck, and luck with art.

AGATHON; QUOTED BY ARISTOTLE

What is he saying here?

Maybe it's that so much in art (and life) is at first a mistake, or an accident, or happenstance. But it's the artist who *recognizes* its beauty and value.

Maybe.

May 15

It is the privilege of adults to give advice. It is the privilege of youth not to listen. Both avail themselves of their privileges, and the world rocks along.

D. SUTTON

One of the things you notice as you age is that so much of life has been done before, said before, lived before. Very little is really new.

But the world rocks along . . .

May 16

Life contains but two tragedies.
One is not to get your heart's desire;
The other is to get it.

SOCRATES

Your greatest strength is also your greatest weakness.

So much of life is a paradox.

May 17

If one is master of one thing and understands one thing well, one
has at the same time insight into and understanding of many
things.

VINCENT VAN GOGH

Did you ever notice that about people?

About yourself?

If one is very good at her work, she is probably very good
at many things.

Doesn't seem quite fair . . . does it?

May 18

To be enlightened is simply to be

absolutely,

unconditionally,

intimate

with this moment.

No more. No less.

SCOTT MORRISON

Succinct.

Now.

And now . . .

May 19

Art happens—no hovel is safe from it, no prince may depend on it, the vastest intelligence cannot bring it about.

J. M. WHISTLER

Always be on the lookout—for art.

Especially where you least expect it.

Then enjoy it, appreciate it.

May 20

What potent blood hath modest May.

RALPH WALDO EMERSON

Why is May strong, Mr. Emerson?

(What's your answer?)

"Potent blood" and "modesty"—a compelling combination.

May 21

Whenever possible,

Avoid eating in a hurry.

Even at home,

Don't gobble up your food.

Eating is an act of holiness.

It requires full presence of mind.

REBBE NACHMAN OF BRESLOV

There is no moment of time, no activity of human life, that does not profit from mindfulness.

Bring mindfulness to the day-to-day acts of your life—

such as eating, or . . .

May 22

Correct handling of flowers refines the personality.

BOKUYO TAKEDA

That might include the art of Ikebana?

Or showing appreciation for the wildflowers a child presents to you?

Or maybe simply arranging gift-flowers in a vase?

All are ways of refining your personality.

May 23

All of our greatest traditions, religious, contemplative and artistic, say that you must learn how to be alone—and have a relationship with silence. It is difficult, but can start with just the tiniest quiet moment.

DAVID WHYTE

Being alone: Where are you on that road?

Comfortable with long periods of solitude? Or not so much?

Either way, give yourself an "alone moment" right now, even if there are others around. Even the tiniest moment can deepen your mindful awareness of now.

May 24

Art enables us to find ourselves and lose ourselves at the same time.

THOMAS MERTON

Find yourself in art . . .

Lose yourself in art . . .

Spend a lot of time with a single work of art you like.

Find.

Lose.

May 25

Spring is the time of year when it is summer in the sun and winter in the shade.

CHARLES DICKENS

Learn to notice (and create) the times of *both . . . and*

Rather than *either . . . or.*

May 26

If we go down into ourselves, we find that we possess exactly what we desire.

SIMONE WEIL

. . . and often exactly what we need as well.

Going down

into yourself,

deeper, deeper . . .

May 27

A deluge of words and a drop of sense.

JOHN RAY

Often

there is

great art, great wisdom

in saying

nothing.

May 28

The single most powerful element of youth is our inability to know what's impossible.

ADAM BRAUN

This from a young CEO of a non-profit.

A contemporary way of saying

"Beginner's mind"?

May 29

Art at its most significant is a Distant Early Warning System that can be relied upon to tell the old culture what is beginning to happen to it.

MARSHALL MCLUHAN

Spend some time in a museum of modern art.

See what's in store for us?

Give it a try.

May 30

Absolutely unmixed attention is prayer.

SIMONE WEIL

Does this make sense to you—whether you pray or not?

Why? How?

Why not?

May 31

Spring passes and one remembers one's innocence . . .

YOKO ONO

As we head into summer, your year has spent a quarter of itself, and can no longer call itself innocent—it's seen a few things.

Will your summer be better off for it?

Part 2

Summer and Early Adulthood

June

Friends, Social Life, and Leisure

June 1

Occasionally I have come across a last patch of snow on top of a mountain in late May or June. There's something very powerful about finding snow in summer.

ANDY GOLDSWORTHY

The surprise, joy—and power—of the unexpected. This shouldn't be here. But it *is* here!

May summer bring you unexpected joys—a snowy patch in the mountains, a friend where there wasn't one, a gift from nowhere . . .

June 2

Consider the question: "How are you?" or "How ya doin?" or "How've you been?" or even "S'up?"

You've asked it—and will ask it again. It's been asked of you many times.

A simple formula of greeting? Do you ever expect to get—or give—an honest, more complete answer?

When? Why?

Be mindful of the question.

June 3

Don't look back. Something may be gaining on you.

SATCHEL PAIGE

. . . and don't look ahead, because there may be nothing there. And even if there is something there, you can't be sure what it is.

Just now.

June 4

The love of our neighbor in all its fullness simply means being
able to say, "What are you going through?"

SIMONE WEIL

Because it implies:

> First, that you care;
>
> That you are open to the life of another;
>
> And that you are available.
>
> No small things.

June 5

Summer is a promissory note signed in June, its long days spent
and gone before you know it . . .

HAL BORLAND

"My, how time flies!" If there is a classic cliché, this is it.

And yet . . . time doesn't actually move quicker now,
slower later.

It's us!

Quiet times this summer will slow time down.

June 6

When I dance, I dance; when I sleep, I sleep; yes, and when I walk alone in a beautiful summer orchard, if my thoughts drift to far-off matters . . . I lead them back again to the walk, the orchard . . . to myself.

MICHEL DE MONTAIGNE

Mindfulness belongs to no specific time, to no specific religion or spiritual system, to no specific place, but to the whole human family—in all times and places . . .

Like you . . .

Right now and . . .

Next year . . . and

June 7

"We could do it, you know."

"What?"

"Leave the district. Run off. Live in the woods. You and I, we could make it."

SUZANNE COLLINS, The Hunger Games

These are the kind of conversations that often come in early adulthood: chucking the "system" and starting over, more simply—while you still can.

Some people actually do it; most don't.

You?

June 8

Go and play. Run around. Build something. Break something. Climb a tree. Get dirty. Get in some trouble. Have some fun.

BROM

Have you ever wanted to say something like this to someone? Maybe some shy or inhibited kid?

Or to yourself?

June 9

A loving person lives in a loving world. A hostile person lives in a hostile world; everyone you meet is your mirror.

KEN KEYES, JR.

So often we see what we expect to see, or what we want to see—not what is actually there. It's filtered through our accumulated experiences.

But of course, seeing another person as a mirror is not the only way to see them.

We can see them as . . .

June 10

Hey, it's summer! Be free and happy and danceful and uninhibited and now-y.

TERRI GUILLEMETS

Nice word, now-y . . .

And danceful.

Have a now-y danceful summer.

June 11

Martha Stewart and Arianna Huffington told an audience of 4,000 entrepreneurs, accountants, and developers to "chill out, unplug, get more sleep, take time away from their computer to plant a tree or collect some eggs."

KATHLEEN PENDER, *San Francisco Chronicle*

Pender added, "No doubt many in the audience were thinking, 'I'll sleep when I'm as rich as you are.'"

I hope they don't act on that thought.

Because *now* is when you need time of peace and quiet, rest and fun.

Now.

June 12

Friendship needs a certain parallelism of life, a community of thought, a rivalry of aim.

HENRY ADAMS

Unpacking that sentence . . .

Parallelism of life: Friendship must fit into the life you've chosen?

Community of thought: Your thoughts are related to your friend's?

Rivalry of aim: There's some competition involved?

What does friendship need for you?

June 13

I do everything on my phone, as a lot of people do.

MARK ZUCKERBERG

I think he doesn't do *everything* on his phone (allow him hyperbole), but he probably does everything that's possible on it. And that's a lot.

But if we hardly ever put our phones down, we risk losing contact with our inner selves.

Chances are your phone is with you right now. Is it on?

Can it help you live in the moment? Consider.

June 14

If you press me to say why I loved him, I can say no more than it was because he was he, and I was I.

MICHEL DE MONTAIGNE

Chemistry, it's often called.

We just clicked.

Isn't it great when that happens?

June 15

Sweet, sweet burn of sun and summer wind, and you my friend, my new fun thing, my summer fling.

K. D. LANG

Nothing like a summer romance: sweet, poignant, painful, wonderful, baffling . . .

And so much more.

June 16

The further you get away from yourself, the more challenging it is. Not to be in your comfort zone is great fun.

BENEDICT CUMBERBATCH

It's an attitude to be admired, I believe, and one that leads to success and accomplishment, at least for the popular English actor.

But not so easy for some of us.

And you, outside your comfort zone?

June 17

You can't put off being young until you retire.

PHILIP LARKIN

Well, duh!

Wait a minute. I think a lot of people do that.

No matter how busy, how little money, how little time:

Do it anyway, do it now, while you can.

June 18

You can learn more about a man in one hour of play than in a lifetime of conversation.

PLATO

Come play with me and I'll tell you who you are.

With whom do you play?

What have you learned of them, and they from you?

June 19

I can take care of my enemies all right. But my damn friends,
my goddam friends. They're the ones who keep me walking the
floor nights.

WARREN G. HARDING

I think that means that President Harding had some very
good friends; they were not sugar-coating the truth.

Or maybe not. Maybe his friends were just troublemakers
and envious of his success. So not really friends.

Or some of each?

Your friends?

June 20

The summer night was like a perfection of thought.

WALLACE STEVENS

*Press close, bare-bosomed Night! . . . Press close, magnetic,
nourishing Night . . . Mad, naked, Summer night!*

WALT WHITMAN

Different takes on a summer's night by two American
poets: one a bit heady, the other very embodied.

Whitman's sounds like more fun.

Notice your nights, this summer.

June 21

*What the banker sighs for, the meanest clown may have—
leisure and a quiet mind.*

HENRY DAVID THOREAU

What about a quiet-minded banker and a sighing clown . . . ?

Less likely—but possible.

Leisure and a quiet mind: What treasures! No matter whose.

Yours?

June 22

The go-between wears out a thousand sandals.

JAPANESE PROVERB

The art of compromise—arriving at a mutually acceptable agreement—consists of never giving up. Never!

After a thousand worn-out sandals, or a million . . .

June 23

The best intelligence test is what we do with our leisure.

LAURENCE J. PETER

Based on this standard, how smart are you?

Do you accept this standard?

June 24

Every day most of us spend some moments—often a lot more—waiting: for the bus, or the train, for your kids, for the Internet, for the pot to boil, and so on and on . . .

. . . time to bring your consciousness into the present moment and simply be aware of what you are experiencing.

Maybe first notice what feelings you are having (impatience? worry?) or how your body is right now . . .

Waiting: valuable time.

June 25

Summer is the time when one sheds one's tensions with one's clothes, and the right kind of day is jeweled balm for the battered spirit. A few of those kinds of days and you can become drunk with the belief that all's right with the world.

ADA LOUISE HUXTABLE

What would the "right kind of day" look like for you?

"Shed your tensions" and "shed your clothes" and see.

Naked and relaxed.

Now what?!

June 26

From desire I plunge to its fulfillment, where I long once more for desire.

GOETHE

Notice this cycle in your life . . . from desire to fulfillment, to desire again . . .

It's never-ending, completely human.

Can be life-defeating, like addiction.

Can be life-giving, like generosity.

June 27

To be social is to be forgiving.

ROBERT FROST

If I die, I forgive you. If I recover, we'll see.

SPANISH PROVERB

Frost states a social truth that we have all experienced: Forgiveness often holds things together.

But the Spanish proverb certainly has a ring of truth.

June 28

Friends are the family you choose.

JESS C. SCOTT

It's often in young adulthood that the realization of the importance of friends hits home.

Think of your friends . . .

Now think of someone you would like to become your friend . . .

So?

June 29

It's important to our friends to believe that we are unreservedly frank with them, and important to friendship that we are not.

MIGNON MCLAUGHLIN

Oh, yes. It's important not to say some things to my friend.

Equally important that she not say some things to me.

(Oh? What things?!)

June 30

It's summer and time for wandering . . .

KELLIE ELMORE

Any plans for some wandering this summer?

Yes? Good.

No? Too bad.

Wandering: aimless, slow, or pointless movement; not keeping a rational or sensible course.

July

Intellectual Life and Culture

July 1

If the first of July be rainy weather.

It will rain, more or less, four weeks together.

ENGLISH PROVERB

Predicting the weather has improved as a science, but it's a long way from perfect. Weather has its way.

Climate is having its way as well.

You and climate change: what?

July 2

We should take care not to make the intellect our god; it has, of course, powerful muscles, but no personality.

ALBERT EINSTEIN

The cool, heady intellect can soar—amazingly

Or dive-bomb—disastrously

It always needs its partner, the heart.

July 3

Civilization is just a slow process of learning to be kind.

CHARLES L. LUCAS

Succinct.

Accurate.

Insightful.

Profound.

July 4

A thought for the day:

True patriotism hates injustice in its own land more than any-where else.

CLARENCE DARROW

When self-criticism becomes unpatriotic, beware.

"My country, right or wrong!"

To love, yes. To honor? Not always?

July 5

Summer afternoon—summer afternoon: to me those have always been the two most beautiful words in the English language.

HENRY JAMES

They are words that speak not only of completely free time . . .

But of no bothersome responsibilities to invade your pleasure . . .

Just free to play. Free to play.

July 6

Progress of civilization is the ever-widening circle of those whom we do not kill.

MARGARET MEAD

We're still living in a world of "ethnic cleansings" . . .

Which has been supported by leaders who say they believe in democracy.

It's always helpful to remember that the world is crazy.

July 7

I harbored a lot of resentment as a teenager and as a young adult. I still have a problem with authority. I am trying to listen!

NIKKI SIXX

An effective way to respond to authority:

Maybe ask some questions, but then just listen carefully.

Only then obey

or disobey.

July 8

It is difficult to produce a television documentary that is both incisive and probing when every twelve minutes one is interrupted by twelve dancing rabbits singing about toilet paper.

ROD SERLING

It's clear in a capitalistic system that "someone has to pay for it."

Whoever pays generally has the power.

As often as not, it's advertising.

So which comes out better: "decisive and probing" or selling more stuff?

July 9

I hate intellectuals. They are from the top down. I am from the bottom up.

FRANK LLOYD WRIGHT

But Mr. Wright, you should know better. Dualism rarely works out well.

It's both: from the top down *and* from the bottom up.

Turns out best for all of us.

July 10

I am summer, come to lure you away from your computer . . . come dance on my fresh grass, dig your toes into my beaches.

ORIANA GREEN

So we're well into July. Have you answered summer? Have you come into contact with fresh grass or sand yet?

If yes, don't stop now.

If no, when?

July 11

Preservation of one's own culture does not require contempt or disrespect for other cultures.

CESAR CHAVEZ

This is of course obvious, a truism.

And yet . . .

Multiculturalism: a good contemporary word.

July 12

My body has certainly wandered a good deal, but I have an uneasy suspicion that my mind has not wandered enough.

NOËL COWARD

Really? I should have thought his mind was a great wanderer, judging by the music he turned out. But I have no way of judging that, do I?

Any "uneasy suspicions" in your head?

Wanderlust is a virtue—in or out of your head.

July 13

Hip-hop offers new ways of seeing and understanding what it means to be black at this pivotal time in history.

TODD BOYD

There's really nothing like hip-hop, its rata-tat-tat cadence, its imaginative rhyming, its overall insistence on attention.

What music helps you see in "new ways"?

July 14

Toutes nos passions reflètent les étoiles.

All of our passions reflect the stars.

VICTOR HUGO

Allons enfants de la Patrie,
Le jour de gloire est arrivé!
Arise, children of the Fatherland,
The day of glory has arrived!

LA MARSEILLAISE

Patriotism has gotten us into—and out of—a lot of trouble.

Your patriotism, on a scale from one to ten?

Want it higher? Lower?

July 15

A man says a lot of things in summer he doesn't mean in winter.

PATRICIA BRIGGS

My hunch is that "a man" in this statement is not sexist (and thus should be "a man or a woman") but intentional and specific.

Are men more fickle than women? It seems to be what the statement implies?

July 16

Anglo-American culture seems to be governed by the perverse belief that portrayals of the body's abuse or destruction are harmless . . . while those that show the body in pleasure act like poison.

WALTER KENDRICK

I don't think any observant person could disagree with this. Violent torture and murder are everywhere in our entertainment, but we have strict censures for sexuality.

What's that about?

July 17

The "silly question" is the first intimation of some totally new development.

ALFRED NORTH WHITEHEAD

So often, it seems, what appears to be silly turns out to be anything but.

So don't hesitate with that comment,

even if it turns out to be just silly.

July 18

What sets worlds in motion is the interplay of differences, their attractions and repulsions.

OCTAVIO PAZ

No culture can live, if it attempts to be exclusive.

MAHATMA GANDHI

Conformity and consistency and compliance are what we are most comfortable with.

Diversity, however, is what we find most commonly in the world. It's where life is.

July 19

I am a writer who came from a sheltered life. A sheltered life can be a daring life as well. For all serious daring comes from within.

EUDORA WELTY

So many people, like Welty, have had a strong, lasting influence on the world's culture from small and hidden places.

It's the inner life.

It's always the inner life.

Go in.

July 20

What good is the warmth of summer, without the cold of winter to give it sweetness.

JOHN STEINBECK

. . . or the warmth of friendship, without the cold of loneliness?

Or the warmth of home, without the cold of homelessness?

Or . . .

July 21

Believe those who are seeking the truth.

Doubt those who have found it.

ANDRÉ GIDE

Truth-seeking never ends.

If the seeking ends because someone has found it,
watch out.

Let's keep on seeking, and find other seekers.

July 22

Anyone who has the power to make you believe in absurdities
has the power to make you commit injustices.

VOLTAIRE

How many times in history has this been proven!

Believing in absurdities, however, is a very easy thing to
do. A very human thing to do.

Watch out for absurdities. Any hanging out near you?

July 23

Culture is the habit of being pleased with the best and knowing why.

HENRY VAN DYKE

It's that "knowing why" part that's interesting.

It reminds me that it is always important to know why I am pleased.

For a moment: Identify why your pleasures are your pleasures.

July 24

The most important part of teaching is to teach what it is to know.

SIMONE WEIL

When we teach (our kids, for example), can we also teach them what it means to know something? How do you do that?

This, it seems to me, is very difficult.

July 25

Deep summer is when laziness finds respectability.

SAM KEEN

Hey, it's the end of July. You don't need any excuses to laze around a bit. Just hang out. Some iced tea. Do nothing.

Will you?

Or maybe more appropriately, can you?

July 26

If art is to nourish the roots of our culture, society must set the artist free to follow his vision wherever it takes him.

JOHN F. KENNEDY

Or her.

Artists are the mirrors. Don't fool with the mirrors.

Look at art.

See you, and me, and all of us.

July 27

A sudden, bold, and unexpected question doth many times surprise a man and lay him open.

FRANCIS BACON

One of life's pleasures is to observe a wily politician totally thrown off base by an innocent question that lays him or her open.

Is that *schadenfreude*?

So be it.

July 28

Anyone interested in the world generally can't help being interested in young adult culture—in the music, the bands, the books, the fashions, and the way in which the young adult community develops its own language.

MARGARET MAHY

It is not at all uncommon to read how much people from other countries hate and disapprove of the USA, while at the same time they are fully accepting of the culture—"music, bands, books, fashions" of our young adults.

Who do you call Ambassador?

July 29

The whole of life lies in the verb seeing.

PIERRE TEILHARD DE CHARDIN

The Jesuit anthropologist saw a lot—and wrote about it. His expression here symbolizes that indeed he saw "too much" and thus was silenced by his church.

Too much truth is too often too scary to too many. Especially to authority.

July 30

Peeling pears—
sweet juice drips
from the knife blade

MASAOKA SHIKI

Haiku poetry is so . . . What? Uncomplicated? Simple? Refreshing? Insightful?

And relaxing.

Try your hand? Just three lines.

July 31

Culture is on the horns of this dilemma: if profound it must remain rare, if common it must become mean.

GEORGE SANTAYANA

So maybe it's an important work to advance the profound (the beautiful, the noble, the generous, etc.) and make it . . .

Common, everyday, expected.

Why not?

August

Family and Family Life

August 1

Anne Frank penned her last entry into her diary on this date in 1944:

I'll keep on trying to find a way of becoming what I would like to be, and what I could be, if . . . there weren't any other people living in the world.

Ah, other people, yes!

But she will keep on trying . . .

Whatever it is we are trying to find . . .

Whatever it is we need, or want . . .

We are all encouraged by the example of this fifteen-year-old girl.

August 2

In every conceivable manner, the family is link to our past,
bridge to our future.

ALEX HALEY

Yes, family is "where we come from." Good, bad, or indifferent—probably a little of each—and whence we are launched into life . . .

And that's where we take over . . .

August 3

Happiness is having a large, loving, caring, close-knit family.
In another city.

GEORGE BURNS

Is there any family that is not a mixed blessing?

Is there any family that is not in some way dysfunctional?

We work with what we've got.

August 4

What can you do to promote world peace?
Go home and love your families.

MOTHER TERESA

Enormous challenges—both world peace and loving your family.

Make the connections.

August 5

Do what we can, summer will have its flies.

RALPH WALDO EMERSON

. . . and its mosquitoes, and poison ivy, and prickly heat, and evenings too hot to sleep . . . and . . .

But what about a perfect, warm August evening, with a soft breeze . . . ? Ahhhh!

August 6

The greatest thing in family life is to take a hint when a hint is intended—and not to take a hint when a hint isn't intended.

ROBERT FROST

Subtle but profound, the poet's advice.

"Take a hint!" or "Get a clue!" When you hear those words, you know you've probably missed something.

But now, just be still . . .

August 7

Come, come, whoever you are. Wanderer, worshiper, lover of leaving. It doesn't matter. Ours is not a caravan of despair. Come, even if you have broken your vows a thousand times. Come, yet again, come, come.

RUMI

If only all families, and family-like groups, operated on the principle of inclusion!

What a different world it would be!

How life-giving it is to say—and to mean—"come, join us, you're one of us."

I bet you'll have a chance to say something like that soon.

August 8

A family is a place where principles are hammered and honed on the anvil of everyday living.

CHARLES R. SWINDOLL

I guess that's where all the dents, and dings, and cuts, and bruises come from—

The wounds of living in a family. Notice them—then get on with it.

August 9

I am the baby of the family, and I always will be. I am actually very happy to have that position.

JANET JACKSON

As well she should be; they often get the best treatment, don't they?

What's your position in the family order?

Its effects?

August 10

Summer-induced stupidity.

That was the diagnosis.

AIMEE FRIEDMAN

There comes a time when there simply is no other way to explain something you've said or done.

The seasons are even interchangeable in this regard.

Been there?

August 11

Parents need all the help they can get. The strongest as well as the most fragile family requires a vital network of social supports.

BERNICE WEISSBOURD

"It takes a village to raise a child." We hear it a lot.

Your village? Did you have one growing up?

Are you part of one now?

August 12

You can kiss your family goodbye and put miles between you,
but at the same time you carry them with you in your heart,
your mind, your stomach . . .

FREDERICK BUECHNER

They are always with us—especially, it seems, in the
stomach!

Welcome or not; helpful or harmful.

And you too are being carried, or have been carried.

August 13

Every child should have a loving adult in their lives. And that's
not always a biological parent or family member. It may be a
friend or neighbor. Oftentimes it is a teacher.

JOE MANCHIN

Can you bring to mind a teacher who cared?

A generous or caring aunt or uncle?

A loving neighbor?

"Thanks!"

August 14

Even though the forms of family life have changed dramatically, the central importance of family and the satisfaction with family life is as strong as it ever was.

PEW RESEARCH CENTER

Family configurations are changing quickly: One-parent families, same-sex parent families, blended families, chosen families, and so on.

The one constant is the desire: however you can get a family (love, support, help, encouragement, fun), get it!

Think of yours a moment—the one you came from, that you helped to create, that you are a part of.

August 15, 1969

Woodstock began on this date in a field near Yasgur's farm in Bethel, New York. The three-day concert featured twenty-four rock bands and drew a crowd of more than 300,000 young people. The event came to symbolize the counterculture of the 1960s.

Woodstock was *the moment* for many of that generation— whether you were there or not—to take a step toward independence from one's family. "Doing your own thing . . ."

. . . with varying results.

A similar moment or event for you?

August 16

Sister is probably the most competitive relationship within the family, but once the sisters are grown, it becomes the strongest relationship.

MARGARET MEAD

This seems an arbitrary opinion, no? Sibling relations are not so easy to predict.

One thing, though, I believe Ms. Mead got right: they often change over time.

August 17

Homegrown tomatoes, homegrown tomatoes
What would life be like without homegrown tomatoes?

GUY CLARK

Is there anything more delicious than a beautiful, big, red, ripe, August tomato? Or maybe for you it's corn or berries or some other savory fruit of summer.

Anticipate now.

Soon: taste!

August 18

Compared to teens who have two or fewer family dinners per week, those who have five or more are at least half as likely to have used tobacco, alcohol, or marijuana, and are less likely to say they would try these substances in the future.

THE NATIONAL CENTER ON
ADDICTION AND SUBSTANCE ABUSE

It's an important place, the family dinner table—to learn who we are, where we come from, what's expected of us, and how to deal with each other.

Interacting with each other.

Pass the potatoes . . . please.

August 19

Who of us is mature enough for offspring before the offspring themselves arrive? The value of marriage is not that adults produce children but that children produce adults.

PETER DE VRIES

Parenting has to be the most obvious case of learning on the job, or "on-the-job training." But somehow, some way, most of us muddle through.

And then start the whole process over again.

August 20

Shall I compare thee to a summer's day?

WILLIAM SHAKESPEARE

And then he does—compare his love to a summer's day, that is—in "Sonnet 18."

"Thou art more lovely and more temperate," he says, and lots more.

A poem to your love?

August 21

The most important thing a father can do for his children is to love their mother.

THEODORE HESBURGH

And, by extension, for the mother to love the father, the one parent to love the other, and the single parent to be loving . . .

No?

To grow up in an atmosphere of love is a pretty great thing.

August 22

'Twas brillig, and the slithy toves

　　Did gyre and gimble in the wabe:

All mimsy were the borogoves,

　　And the mome raths outgrabe.

LEWIS CARROLL, "Jabberwocky"

The family, often like the Lewis Carroll poem, "Jabber-wocky," does not always make sense, is often difficult or impossible to explain or understand.

It can also be like a magical mystery tour!

But whatever it is, the family always seems to be full of life, challenges, and even sometimes fun!

August 23

Nothing has a stronger influence psychologically on their environment, and especially on their children, than the unlived life of the parent.

CARL JUNG

Don't limit a child to your own learning, for he was born in another time.

RABBINIC SAYING

Fortunate the family that understands these insights and allows the children to follow what they would follow, be what they would be.

With maybe a little pushing here and holding back there?

Probably.

August 24

Meditation is the act of checking in on yourself . . . You just drop in. It turns out to be the simplest thing in the world. There's nothing particularly mystical or magical about it. And it's readily available to us.

JON KABAT-ZINN

It is, of course, what you're doing here.

Keeping up with yourself.

Trying to make sure you don't miss important stuff.

Paying attention.

August 25

When summer opens, I see how fast it matures, and fear it will be short; but after the heats of July and August, I am reconciled, like one who has had his swing, to the cool of autumn.

RALPH WALDO EMERSON

Has it happened yet, the first sign of the cool of autumn?

Often it is noticed in late August as "something in the air"—a slight shiver, a sign of things to come.

Notice it when it comes.

August 26

Nobody, who has not been in the interior of a family, can say what the difficulties of any individual of that family may be.

JANE AUSTEN

. . . which is a nice encouragement to try not to judge. Because often we really don't know what goes on in a family, what challenges they have, what burdens they bear.

Far from judgment, close to encouragement—it's a good place to be.

August 27

Feelings of worth can flourish only in an atmosphere where individual differences are appreciated, mistakes are tolerated, communication is open, and rules are flexible—the kind of atmosphere found in a nurturing family.

VIRGINIA SATIR

From a wise professional on family life comes a definition of an ideal, nurturing family.

But I don't think any family embodies these characteristics 100 percent.

So "feelings of worth" can come from less-than-perfect families.

Whew!

August 28

One would be less in danger

From the wiles of a stranger

If one's own kin and kith

Were more fun to be with.

OGDEN NASH

True, you don't get to choose your kin. They are given to you, no questions asked, and if you have fun with them, lucky you!

If you don't have fun with your kith, however, don't blame your kin.

August 29

The dark, uneasy world of family life—where the greatest can fail and the humblest succeed.

RANDALL JARRELL

Is the family a dark, uneasy world? Too often, I think it is. But in a place where things are always in a state of getting worked out, that's a likely result.

Many of us have seen the happy if unexpected result of a dark, uneasy family giving life to a wonderful and shining child.

August 30

This was one of those perfect New England days in late summer where the spirit of autumn takes its first stealing flight, like a spy, through the ripening countryside, and, with feigned sympathy for those who droop with August heat, puts her cool cloak of bracing air about leaf and flower and human shoulders.

SARAH ORNE JEWETT

What a fine English sentence!

What a beautiful sentiment!

Thank you, Sarah.

August 31

August rain: the best of summer is gone, and the new fall not yet born.

The odd uneven time.

SYLVIA PLATH

Let's give the poet the last words for August: The odd uneven time.

How is it a bit odd for you?

How uneven?

Part 3

Autumn and Middle Age

September

Health, Wellness, and Illness

September 1

By all these lovely tokens September days are here

With summer's best of weather and autumn's best of cheer.

HELEN HUNT JACKSON

What are your "tokens" of the arrival of fall? Bring to mind a few of the symbols of autumn that work for you—places, events, persons, weather.

Then simply notice and enjoy the unique flavors, sights, and sounds that surround you this fall.

September 2

*Health is infinite and expansive . . . and reaches out to be filled
with the fullness of the world;*

*Disease is finite and reductive . . . and endeavors to reduce the
world to itself.*

OLIVER SACKS

The expansiveness of the world that is brought by health
combines with the process of reduction and loss that are
part of illness.

What balance of the two are you feeling at the moment?

September 3

*The only way to keep your health is to eat what you don't want,
drink what you don't like, and do what you'd rather not.*

MARK TWAIN

While he certainly conveys an exaggerated attitude we can
all relate to, I include Twain's comment as an example of
"the old thinking."

At least that's my take on it.

Yours?

September 4

To safeguard one's health at the cost of too strict a diet is a tiresome illness indeed.

FRANÇOIS DE LA ROCHEFOUCAULD

Most of us have had our time with diets.

Fear of food is not good.

Eat everything (you like).

Moderation.

Again.

September 5

On a bare branch
A crow is perched—
Autumn evening

MATSUO BASHŌ

Picture it.

That's all.

A simple moment in time.

A "now."

September 6

I was sick and you visited me . . .

MATTHEW 25:36

. . . or otherwise thought about me, did not forget me,
cooked for me, ran errands—and, perhaps most impor-
tantly, let me know in some way you cared.

The deepest thanks are reserved for you.

September 7

Finally it has penetrated my thick skull. This life—this moment—is no dress rehearsal. This is it!

FLETCHER KNEBEL

A great mid-life insight,

which maybe we can't even achieve before mid-life.

(This is not a dress rehearsal!)

September 8

Before undergoing a surgical operation arrange your temporal affairs. You may live.

AMBROSE BIERCE

Nothing like a serious operation or illness to concentrate the mind.

The parts of our life suddenly unscramble and are re-arranged quite clearly by order of importance.

An undesired gift?

September 9

One in four adults—approximately 61.5 million Americans—experiences mental illness in a given year.

NATIONAL ALLIANCE ON MENTAL ILLNESS

That's a lot of us. Here's another way to look at it:

Mental health problems do not affect three or four out of every five persons, but one out of one.

WILLIAM MENNINGER

We are all touched by mental illness—one way or another.

How are you affected?

September 10

We achieve inner health only through forgiveness—the forgiveness not only of others but also of ourselves.

JOSHUA LOTH LIEBMAN

It does seem much easier to forgive others, doesn't it—it often just seems to happen on its own—when we have already forgiven ourselves.

"For what?" you might ask . . .

September 11

An attack on one is an attack on all.

NATO SECRETARY GENERAL LORD ROBERTSON

The first time I realized I was patriotic was after September 11th.

CLAIRE DANES

The grief endures.

For all of us.

Be still.

Only silence.

September 12

It is no measure of health to be well adjusted to a profoundly sick society.

JIDDU KRISHNAMURTI

That's a challenging saying, but one I believe worth attending.

Indeed, it can be a sign of mental and spiritual health to be out of sync with the sick elements of society.

Out-of-sync you?

September 13

When we are sick, our virtues and our vices are held in abeyance.

LUC DE CLAPIERS, *marquis de Vauvenargues*

Because feeling lousy is all we can think about.

We're not good. We're not bad.

We're sick.

As they say, "the tongue ever seeks the aching tooth."

September 14

Optimistic lies have such an immense therapeutic value that a doctor who cannot tell them convincingly has mistaken his profession.

BERNARD SHAW

Hope is an essential ingredient in maintaining recovery.

And at times that hope turns out to be well-founded

and not a lie at all.

So the doctor's "lie" wasn't a lie?

September 15

Middle age is when you have a choice of two temptations and choose the one that will get you home earlier.

ANONYMOUS

A quiet evening at home.

What an immense world of values that implies!

Maybe "peace and quiet" is one of them.

And you really don't have to be middle-aged.

September 16

In the late evening, from mid- to late fall, Cassiopeia can be seen in the night sky as a "W" (with one slightly lazy wing) high in the sky. It is a circumpolar constellation, and is on the opposite side of the North Star (Polaris) from the Big Dipper. When Cassiopeia is high in the sky (in the fall), the Big Dipper is low.

Do you know something of the night sky? I hope so.

If not, mid-life is an appropriate time to begin this familiarity.

A rich world awaits you.

September 17

Now in his middle age he began to know that love was neither a state of grace nor an illusion; he saw it as a human act of becoming, a condition that was invented and modified moment by moment and day by day, by the will and the intelligence and the heart.

JOHN WILLIAMS, *Stoner*

Love:

A human act of becoming

A condition invented and modified

By the will, the intelligence, the heart.

Amen.

September 18

The ability to be in the present moment is a major component of mental wellness.

ABRAHAM MASLOW

Here, mental health and mindfulness

are brought together—close together.

In fact, essentially related.

Your meditation encourages mental wellness.

September 19

Her emphasis (in teaching mindfulness) is on noticing moment-to-moment changes around you, from the differences in the face of your spouse across the breakfast table to the variability of your asthma symptoms.

BRUCE GRIERSON (ON ELLEN LANGER)

I believe that noticing is a big part of mindfulness.

Noticing means not simply seeing (or hearing) something, but also allowing what you notice to affect you in some way—

responding in some way.

September 20

In many ways, September feels like the busiest time of the year; the kids go back to school, work piles up after the summer's dog days, and Thanksgiving is suddenly upon us.

BRENÉ BROWN

Really, it's the beginning of the year for many of us—especially if we are or are around students.

Things often start up in the fall.

Do you have any startings this fall?

September 21

After dinner, rest a while.
After supper, walk a mile.

ARABIC PROVERB

The human need for regular exercise is well known—our bodies were built to keep moving.

If you are able-bodied, how do you move your body?

Achieve the balance between rest and movement?

September 22

The autumn equinox occurs today (or the 23rd or even occasionally the 24th). This happens when the sun is directly in line with the earth's equator, projected onto the sky. Day and night are about equally long, with twelve hours of light and twelve hours of darkness.

The days shorten now, and the nights lengthen.

We are part of a moving universe that obeys certain laws.

This is one of them.

You are a citizen of a moving universe.

You can see its movement. Do you ever feel it?

September 23

Sickness is a sort of early old age; it teaches us a diffidence in our earthly state.

ALEXANDER POPE

So sickness acts as a reminder of old age and makes us a bit uncomfortable, careful, and even distrustful of our "earthly state" . . .

. . . as well we should be.

No?

September 24

There are some remedies worse than the disease.

PUBLILIUS SYRUS

This has been going on for a long time; Syrus lived in the first century BCE.

Pain, illness, and discomfort, on the one hand

and the medicine that gets rid of them, on the other.

It can be a difficult choice.

September 25

It's never too late to have a fling
For autumn is just as nice as spring
And it's never too late to fall in love.

SANDY WILSON

So go ahead, fall in love:

With an idea . . .

With a place . . .

With an activity . . .

Or even with someone.

September 26

It's much more important to know what sort of patient has the disease than what sort of disease a patient has.

WILLIAM OSLER

It is? Well, maybe. Certainly both are important.

Mostly, however, we have been concentrating on the disease, and overlooking the diseased.

Whatever the sickness, see the person first.

September 27

The concept of total wellness recognizes that our every thought, word, and behavior affects our greater health and well-being . . . not only emotionally but also physically and spiritually.

GREG ANDERSON

This thought, that action, and those words: They can all make you more or less healthy.

So I guess kindness to others is also kindness to me?

What a concept.

(I think that's been said before.)

September 28

Middle age snuffs out more talent than even wars and sudden deaths do.

RICHARD HUGHES

Middle age is the time when you are often tempted to abandon your more youthful goals and desires, or to "get yours" while the getting is good. Besides, you can begin to get just a bit tired.

It can, however, also be a time to renew old goals, perhaps adjusted as necessary, and continue to get better.

Seems a critical choice.

September 29

*Nothing is more essential in the treatment of serious disease
than the liberation of the patient from panic and foreboding.*

NORMAN COUSINS

The panic and foreboding add to the illness. Cousins,
a writer, is well known for having staved off his own
life-threatening illness by prioritizing humor and laughter.

It worked. He inspired research on the effect of emotions
on health that continues to this day.

September 30

*There is so much beauty in autumn and so much wisdom; so
much separation and so much sorrow!*

MEHMET MURAT İLDAN

Your fall beauty?

Your wisdom?

You feel separated from?

And sad about?

October

Work and Money

October 1

Chicago is an October sort of city, even in the spring.

NELSON ALGREN

"An October sort of city"—maybe moody, a bit melancholic (but not depressed), a place for new beginnings, cozy, friendly (but not overly so), companionable, smart, certainly windy . . .

Your take on an "October sort of city?"

October 2

Some people see things that are and ask, Why? Some people see things that never were and ask, Why not? Some people have to go to work and don't have time for all that.

GEORGE CARLIN

Carlin often cuts right to the core of things: Who has time for all that esoteric clap-trap when most of us have to work all day and attend to home duties the rest of the time?

Would this be your sentiment?

October 3

Give me control of a nation's money and I care not who makes her laws.

M. A. ROTHSCHILD

He who controls the money supply of a nation controls the nation.

JAMES A. GARFIELD

The flood of money that gushes into politics is a pollution of democracy.

THEODORE WHITE

These statements were made in the 1790s, 1850s, and 1960s, respectively.

We're still at it, big-time.

But just for now . . . let it go.

October 4

With hard work, drive, and passion, it's possible to achieve the American dream.

TOMMY HILFIGER

Maybe. At one time in our history.

I know some Millennials who might not agree with this traditional belief.

Or maybe "the American dream" is changing?

October 5

Listen! The wind is rising, and the air is wild with leaves,
We have had our summer evenings, now for October eves!

HUMBERT WOLFE

This is the time of year to settle down in the evening with a good book where it's warm and comfortable, and the howling wind is only a distant sound.

Withdraw for a spell!

October 6

Surround yourself with people who take their work seriously,
but not themselves . . .

COLIN POWELL

For a moment or two think of a few characteristics of
people who do not take themselves too seriously. I bet you
like them.

Then, forget all that—let it go and just be still . . .

. . . in this moment.

October 7

The mid-life crisis hits men harder than women.

SONIA JOHNSON

Around mid-life everyone goes maniac a little bit.

TOM BERENGER

What do you say? Are men "hit harder" than women with middle age?

Or do they just experience it in a different way?

I know some who seem to have never had a mid-life crisis.

(And yes, the word is "maniac" not "manic;" crazy-wild, not overactive.)

October 8

You can have money piled to the ceiling but the size of your funeral is still going to depend on the weather.

CHUCK TANNER

There's a statement that can give you perspective.

Get you back to making priorities.

Even cut you down to size.

October 9

The contemporary form of true greatness lies in a civilization founded on the spirituality of work.

SIMONE WEIL

The phrase "spirituality of work" is challenging to unpack, no?

But I suspect she means that we bring our personal values to bear on the work we do . . .

. . . or something like that?

October 10

October is a fine and dangerous season in America, a wonderful time to begin anything at all.

THOMAS MERTON

October is a dangerous month? The only way I can understand that is by thinking that October is a month of deep emotions; there's just something in the air, something in the transition from summer to winter.

And, of course, anywhere there are strong emotions, there can be danger, risk . . .

Your take on this?

October 11

Don't tell me where your priorities are. Show me where you spend your money and I'll let you know what they are.

JAMES W. FRICK

A budget is a spiritually revealing document.

Take a moment to review, broadly, your own budget.

Is it proportioned the way you really want it?

Want some revision?

October 12

They intoxicate themselves with work so they won't see how they really are.

ALDOUS HUXLEY

Workaholism is a serious problem: always working, or thinking about work.

Whether it's to avoid thinking more deeply about oneself—as Huxley opines—or just picking up the American pace and values . . .

It's time to stop. It ruins health, on all levels.

But maybe this has nothing to do with you . . .

October 13 (Columbus Day)

He stands out among the beacon lights of history as a man of vision dominated by a definite purpose.

JOHN GEORGE JONES

But that's not the only take on Columbus or his Day. Many continue to protest Columbus Day celebrations because of the way he and his crew treated the native peoples they encountered—because how can you discover a land that was already inhabited?

And Columbus likely was not the first non-indigenous person to arrive here; the Vikings were.

Things change, don't they?

October 14

Love and work are the cornerstones of our humanness.

SIGMUND FREUD

*Although Freud said happiness is composed of love and work,
reality often forces us to choose love or work.*

LETTY COTTIN POGREBIN

Lust and learning. That's really all there is, isn't it?

JOHN WILLIAMS

Love and work. Love and work. Since the time of Freud
the Western world has accepted this division of life.

Pogrebin, a contemporary American author and feminist,
and Williams, a novelist, have new insights.

Your love? Your work? The balance?

October 15

There is no season when such pleasant and sunny spots may be lighted on, and produce so pleasant an effect on the feelings, as now in October.

NATHANIEL HAWTHORNE

I admit it: October is my favorite month.

Such variety of weather

Dark as well as light as well as both at once

Warmish chills and cool warmth

Feelings seem to run deeper . . .

Do you have a favorite month?

Which? And why?

October 16

With money in your pocket, you are wise, and you are hand-some, and you sing well too.

JEWISH PROVERB

We tend to pay compliments to rich people, whether they are true or not.

Why? Do we want their money? Their approval?

Silly, isn't it? But all too human.

October 17

My heroes are just everyday people who work hard, are honest, and have integrity.

JORDIN SPARKS

With social media, it seems there is no one who is "everyday" or unsung; they're tweeted or Facebooked or Instagrammed.

But virtue is still its own reward, tweeted or not.

October 18

Of the billionaires I have known, money just brings out the basic traits in them. If they were jerks before they had money, they are simply jerks with a billion dollars.

WARREN BUFFETT

That's such a scary image—"jerks with a billion dollars!"

(I realize that I assume that no billionaires will be reading this book. But just maybe, one might. Hey, if it's you: Please don't be a jerk! Be kind! Be generous! Be smart! We all thank you.)

October 19

I don't think people understand that being poor means you have to work from dawn until dusk just to survive through the day. I think there's some notion that poor people lie about all day not doing anything.

EMMA THOMPSON

Maybe the most challenging thing about poverty is not "not having money;" it's having very little or no power to change your life.

You and poverty: the relationship?

A challenging topic. So spend a moment with it, then let your thoughts go and be still . . .

October 20

There are three things in my life which I really love: God, my family, and baseball. The only problem—once baseball season starts, I change the order around a bit.

AL GALLAGHER

Maybe true, especially in World Series month.

It's good to have a vital interest in sports—our home team. It gives us time away from the heavier things, to yell and scream at "da bums"!

October 21

Gambling generates more revenue than movies, spectator sports, theme parks, cruise ships, and recorded music combined.

CRACKED.COM AND FRONTLINE

This seems an amazing statistic; I checked several sources and it seems to hold up.

That's a lot of hopes and dreams cast upon the sea of chance—which is even stacked against you.

October 22

Housekeeping ain't no joke.

LOUISA MAY ALCOTT

The American writer (of *Little Women*) knew whereof she spoke. She worked as a maid and kept up her family home.

In recent decades housekeeping and homemaking have received more of their due credit as full-time, challenging, and important work.

Why in the world wouldn't they?

Who keeps your home?

October 23

You will spend at least 60 percent of your life working. That includes the time you spend at work, as well as all the time you spend preparing for it, looking for it, commuting to it, and recovering from it on the weekend.

MANIFESTYOURPOTENTIAL.COM

That's more than half your life.

So try to concentrate on the other 40 percent.

October 24

Rest is the sweet sauce of labor.

PLUTARCH

Since the first century (CE) when Plutarch lived, rest has been the reward to labor.

Or has it?

How often during your work day do you rest?

(I can hear you laughing!)

October 25

October is the fallen leaf, but it is also a wider horizon more clearly seen.

HAL BORLAND

It's the time of year to notice leaves. On the tree or off. Blowing in the breeze or raked into piles. Their colors and shapes. How they come and go.

How the horizon can be seen more clearly when there are no leaves on the trees.

Press one in a book. Gather a few in a bunch. Twirl one in your hand as you walk the neighborhood.

October 26

Why is there so much month left at the end of the money?

ANONYMOUS

It always seems to happen. Just when you catch up with the bills and expenses, something unexpected comes along and clobbers you.

Muddling through is perfectly acceptable, you know. It's the "through" part you want to concentrate on, not the "muddling."

October 27

Every person's work, whether it be literature, or music, or pictures, or architecture, or anything else, is always a self-portrait.

SAMUEL BUTLER

When your work speaks for itself, don't interrupt.

HENRY J. KAISER

While you are not what you do,

what you do does offer a reflection of you.

Offer it.

Then, be still.

October 28

*Here comes forty. I'm feeling my age and I've ordered the
Ferrari. I'm going to get the whole mid-life crisis package.*

KEANU REEVES

*Mid-life is the time to let go of an overdominant ego and to con-
template the deeper significance of human existence.*

CARL JUNG

Carl and Keanu might not see eye to eye here—but they
don't have to. Each has his take on it.

Mid-life crisis for you? Long gone? Not yet arrived? In the
middle of it?

A mess? An opportunity? A little of both?

October 29

Do not wait; the time will never be "just right." Start where you stand, and work with whatever tools you may have at your command.

GEORGE HERBERT

October has been called a good time to start something. That's a bit unexpected to me. Seems more like a month of ending.

Oh, maybe it's that too!

Yes, endings imply new beginnings.

October 30

All things on earth point home in old October; sailors to sea, travelers to walls and fences, hunters to field and hollow and the long voice of the hounds, the lover to the love he has forsaken.

THOMAS WOLFE

October is old now and it's time to point for home.

Where is home for you? It may be in a few places. It may be where a certain person is. Or a house. Or a room?

We generally have a few homes in a lifetime.

A favorite?

October 31

Double, double toil and trouble;
Fire burn and cauldron bubble.

WILLIAM SHAKESPEARE, *Macbeth*

We seek to be delivered:
From ghoulies and ghosties
And long-legged beasties
And things that go bump in the night.

Halloween is a time to indulge the dark side. What fun!

Let Edgar Allen Poe lead us out of October:

Deep into the darkness peering, long I stood there,
wondering, fearing,

Doubting, dreaming dreams no mortal ever dared to
dream before.

"THE RAVEN"

Spend some moments in dreaming . . .

November

Science and Religion

November 1

Emily: Do any human beings ever realize life while they live it—every, every minute?

Stage Manager: No. (pause) The saints and poets, maybe they do some.

THORNTON WILDER'S OUR TOWN

The saints and the poets. In other words, people who do their best to live honest and generous lives and people who have expressed themselves through poetry. "Maybe they do some."

But every, *every* minute? I don't think so.

It's still a good ambition, no?

November 2

Al vivo todo le falta, y al muerto todo le sobra.

For the living nothing's enough, for the dead anything's too much.

MEXICAN PROVERB

Today is the Día de los Muertos, the day of the dead, for the Spanish-speaking world, especially Mexico. It's All Souls' Day in some religious traditions.

One of the advantages of thinking about one's death is that you realize, more and more, that now is all you're really sure of—so don't put off.

November 3

In fact a universe like ours with galaxies and stars is actually quite unlikely. If one considers the possible constants and laws that could have emerged, the odds against a universe that has produced life like ours are immense.

STEPHEN HAWKING

But it is the universe we have.

Wonder of wonders! Miracle of miracles!—even if unlikely.

November 4

Formerly, when religion was strong and science was weak, men mistook magic for medicine; now, when science is strong and religion weak, men mistake medicine for magic.

THOMAS SZASZ

Medicine and magic.

Science and mysterious enchantment.

Both are good

for different reasons.

Let's do our best not to confuse them.

November 5

The month of November makes me feel that life is passing more quickly. In an effort to slow it down, I try to fill the hours more meaningfully.

HENRY ROLLINS

How might you fill your hours "more meaningfully"?

Do you even want to?

Got some examples?

November 6

Everything is holy!

Everything is holy!

Everything is holy!

Everyman's an angel!

ALLEN GINSBERG

(And every woman.)

This, from the Beat poet who wrote "Howl"?

Yes.

Well, there you have it. Why not?

November 7

Maturity: among other things, not to hide one's strength out of fear and, consequently, live below one's best.

DAG HAMMARSKJÖLD

I have a hunch that the tendency "to hide one's strength out of fear" is more common than we may think.

Maturity is a good goal for mid-life . . .

November 8

Laid end to end, there are about 60,000 miles of blood vessels in your body.

The heart pumps about 2,000 gallons of blood every day.

A red blood cell makes a complete circuit of your body in 20 seconds.

SCIENCE-FACTS.COM

Take an imaginary ride on one of your red blood cells . . .

Zoom! Zoom!

November 9

Science without religion is lame; religion without science is blind.

ALBERT EINSTEIN

Einstein did not believe in a personal God, and yet he showed a great deal of respect and appreciation for religions, which can, as he intimates above, contribute values and morality to the world of science.

So?

November 10

If Galileo had said in verse that the world moved, the Inquisi-
tion might have let him alone.

THOMAS HARDY

Your Grace, the earth doth spin

Of this I am quite sure.

A poem saves my skin

by feint, as I demure.

Surely true, as well as something to keep in mind. It might
come in handy—when you need to say something . . .
uh . . . sensitive, say it with a poem.

November 11

Every November of my boyhood, we put on red poppies and attended highly patriotic services in remembrance of those who had "given" their lives.

CHRISTOPHER HITCHENS

He puts *given* in quotes.

Hmmm . . .

Some surely were "given"—offered, so to speak.

Others? Who can judge?

November 12

He was of the faith chiefly in the sense that the Church he currently did not attend was Catholic.

KINGSLEY AMIS

Surveys are showing more and more disaffiliation with organized religion. Yet so often the identity sticks.

Your relationship with your faith-at-birth?

Maybe you didn't receive one.

Thus?

November 13

*The means by which we live have outdistanced the ends for
which we live.*

Our scientific power has outrun our spiritual power.

We have guided missiles and misguided men.

MARTIN LUTHER KING, JR.

Science and religion.

Knowledge and spirituality.

Always an uneasy duality.

Keeping up with one another?

Are they supposed to?

November 14

I consider myself a Hindu, Christian, Moslem, Jew, Buddhist,
and Confucian.

MAHATMA GANDHI

"Could he just do that?"

"He did."

"Don't you have to ask someone?"

"Who?"

November 15

Whenever I find myself growing grim about the mouth; when-
ever it is a damp, drizzly November in my soul . . . I account it
high time to get to sea as soon as I can.

HERMAN MELVILLE

Where do you "get to" as quick as you can when you've
become, like a drizzly November, "grim about the mouth?"

To the sea, like Melville?

To the mountains?

Or . . .

November 16

There isn't anything to worry about between science and religion, because the contradictions are just in your own mind . . .

HENRY J. EYRING

Many would agree with the Mormon academic . . . and many would not.

Agree or not, it does seem an important issue.

Or does it?

November 17

The world would be a safer place,
If someone had a plan,
Before exploring Outer Space,
To find the inner man.

E. Y. HARBURG

Going in. Deep.

Going out. Far.

Both are challenging

And often fraught with dangers.

Which of the two kinds of dangers is your
inclination?

November 18

Religion is the art of the poetic.
Science is the art of the provable.
Politics is the art of the possible.

PAUL H. CARR

Carr is a physicist and, in my experience, physics and spirituality are often friends. Perhaps the most notable thing he says is that religion, science, and politics are all art.

November 19

The first scientist to propose the Big Bang Theory was a
Catholic priest: Rev. Georges Lamaître of Belgium in
the 1930s.

SCIENCE-FACTS.COM/WIKIPEDIA

Science is science. Religion is religion.

As Chet Raymo points out, "The science I learned at Notre Dame was the same science that was taught at the University of California at Los Angeles."

November 20

You can't hide your true colors as you approach the autumn of your life.

UNKNOWN

At that time, the book called *Who I Am* has mostly been written . . .

. . . or, if you are not in the "autumn of your life," you are in the middle of writing it

and still mixing your true colors.

November 21

No shade, no shine, no butterflies, no bees,
No fruits, no flowers, no leaves, no birds—November!

THOMAS HOOD

On the other hand, one could make a list of what you do have in November.

Your list?

November 22

The real 1960s began on the afternoon of November 22, 1963. It came to seem that Kennedy's murder opened some maligned trap door in American culture, and the wild bats flapped out.

LANCE MORROW

Wild bats? Well, maybe . . .

But certainly psychedelic butterflies as well!

Bats or butterflies, the 1960s were exciting, influential, and often fun.

November 23

I am a child of the Milky Way. The night is my mother. I am made of the dust of stars. Every atom in my body was forged in a star . . .

CHET RAYMO

Everything that exists—that's everything, including you and me—was present at the Big Bang. So goes the currently accepted theory of our beginnings.

An idea to ponder as you look into the night sky.

November 24

Winter is an etching, spring a watercolor, summer an oil paint-ing and autumn a mosaic of them all.

STANLEY HOROWITZ

Look for the colors of the autumn mosaic in your specific part of the world and notice their appeal, their allure.

November 25

Justice Stewart's wisdom about pornography applies to mid-life, too: tough to define, but you know it when you're in it.

4060MEN.COM

I suppose everyone enters middle age at a different time. To know it exactly, you'd have to know your date of death, wouldn't you?

It can start any time, no?

November 26

Thanksgiving is the fourth Thursday in November.

If the only prayer you ever said in your whole life was "thank you," that would suffice.

MEISTER ECKHART

"Thank you."

"You're welcome" is pretty good too.

November 27

Our Milky Way galaxy is one among billions of galaxies in space.

Stay with each phrase: Milky Way . . .

One of billions . . .

of galaxies.

Something to bring to mind about the moment I want to complain to the waiter who forgot the mayo.

November 28

In mid-life the man wants to see how irresistible he still is to younger women. How they turn their hearts to stone and more or less commit murder of their marriage I just don't know, but they do.

JUSTICE EARL WARREN

Some do.

Many do not.

Some women do too.

Many do not.

No one appointed me judge.

November 29

Q: Why can't you trust atoms?

A: They make up everything.

Arrrgh!

Devoutly to be hoped for: the very last thing to lose in life will be your sense of humor.

The gift of laughter is a fine gift!

November 30

Fallen leaves lying on the grass in the November sun bring more happiness than the daffodils.

CYRIL CONNOLLY

What about you? Daffodils or fallen leaves?

Let the images of each lead you to reverie . . .

. . . and to December.

Part 4

Winter and Old Age

December

Dying and Death

December 1

*How did it get so late so soon? It's night before it's afternoon.
December is here before it's June. My goodness how the time has
flewn. How did it get so late so soon?*

DR. SEUESS

The end of the year is at hand, with the holidays and all
the frenzy they often bring.

What are your expectations this year?

Prepare now.

Then, be still.

December 2

Almost everything—all external expectations, all pride, all fear of embarrassment or failure—these things just fall away in the face of death, leaving only what is truly important. Remembering that you are going to die is the best way I know to avoid the trap of thinking you have something to lose.

STEVE JOBS

Remembering death, perhaps unexpectedly, enhances life.

It's ancient wisdom.

Forever new.

December 3

The privilege of a lifetime is being who you are.

JOSEPH CAMPBELL

Every person dies—not every person really lives.

WILLIAM ROSS WALLACE

Happy the person who, at the end of life, can feel a degree of satisfaction, peace, and serenity.

In the meantime—during your life, that is—

pay as much attention as you can.

December 4

When the game is over, the king and the pawn go back into the same box.

ITALIAN PROVERB

The once-powerful and the once-powerless snuggle, side by side, finally showing what they always were—

on one level, anyway.

The great equalizer: death.

December 5

Lighting one candle
from another—
Winter night

YOSA BUSON

A striking and charming winter's image.

Imagine it for a moment.

December 6

Today is the feast of St. Nicholas—who eventually became Santa Claus—and the patron saint of children, bankers, scholars, orphans, laborers, travelers, merchants, judges, paupers, marriageable maidens, students, sailors, victims of judicial mistakes, captives, perfumers, pawnbrokers, thieves, and murderers.

Born in 270 BCE in Greece (now Turkey), what a big soul he must have been!

Everybody wanted him.

I wonder why?

(Maybe it's because generosity is hard to resist.)

December 7

Old age is like everything else. To make a success of it, you've got to start young.

THEODORE ROOSEVELT

A kind old man was invariably a kind young man;

a wise old woman, a wise young one.

Can a leopard change its spots?

Just now.

December 8

My poetry doesn't change from place to place—it changes with the years. It's very important to be one's age. You get ideas you have to turn down—"I'm sorry, no longer"; "I'm sorry, not yet."

W. H. AUDEN

How often we might be wise to say those words: "I'm sorry, no longer" or "I'm sorry, not yet." And yet we don't.

Act your age—whatever age you are, and whatever that means to you.

Something to be fervently hoped for.

December 9

One day your life will flash before your eyes.
Make sure it's worth watching.

GERARD WAY

And especially make sure that it's your life that's flashing—not someone else's idea of your life.

Oh, my! That would be sad indeed.

December 10

I am ready to meet my Maker. Whether my Maker is prepared for the ordeal of meeting me is another matter.

WINSTON CHURCHILL

Seems to me one would have to have a big ego to quip like this, no?

But then, big egos are often necessary and effective in times of crisis when there's need for leadership.

You and big egos—what's the relationship?

December 11

The answer to old age is to keep one's mind busy and go right on with one's life as if it were interminable. I always admired Chekhov for building a new house when he was dying.

LEON EDEL

"To go right on with one's life" rather than what?

Stop and wait? No!

Go backwards? Not really!

Give up? Too gloomy!

December 12

Do not go gentle into that good night,
Old age should burn and rave at close of day;
Rage, rage against the dying of the light.

DYLAN THOMAS

The oft-quoted words of the Welsh poet urge us to fight dying, "rage against" it!

But then, is there a moment to let it come?

December 13

Grow old along with me!
The best is yet to be,
The last of life, for which the first was made . . .

ROBERT BROWNING

Ah, Browning. Take you back to high school English class?

The words, immortal as they are to the English-speaking world, encapsulate almost perfectly the enthusiasm and optimism of youth.

December 14

Growing old is like being increasingly penalized for a crime you have not committed.

ANTHONY POWELL

Well, Mr. Powell, that's one way to look at it. Strindberg says that "growing old is not nice—but it's interesting."

So let's look for the interesting parts.

December 15

One should never make one's debut in a scandal.
One should reserve that to give interest to one's old age.

OSCAR WILDE

Scandal is one way to make old age "interesting."

I think I'd rather have it earlier.

You?

(Maybe not at all.)

December 16

Youth, large, lusty, loving—

Youth, full of grace, force, fascination.

Do you know that old age may come after you with equal grace, force, fascination?

WALT WHITMAN

So old age may come after me?

With force?!

Am I ready for that?

December 17

It's pretty much impossible to feel anger at someone for driving too slowly in front of you . . . when you've just come from sanding your own coffin.

JEFFREY M. PIEHLER

Piehler built his own coffin from scratch, of pine boards.

Far from being morbid, keeping the thought of your own death close to your consciousness can be a life-giving act.

Isn't it about keeping priorities—making sure first things are first?

December 18

One kind word can warm three winter months.

JAPANESE PROVERB

Oh, yes!

I bet it can warm an even longer time!

A lifetime?

December 19

I must be getting absent-minded. Whenever I complain that things aren't what they used to be, I always forget to include myself.

GEORGE BURNS

When does it begin? That feeling that you are not what you used to be?

Maybe around adolescence?

December 20

Now, now my good man, this is no time for making enemies.

VOLTAIRE

This is the deathbed response of the eighteenth-century
French philosopher to a priest asking that he renounce
Satan.

It seems to me the epitome of wit.

And also something to think about.

December 21

Though my soul may set in darkness
it will rise in perfect light.
I have loved the stars too fondly
to be fearful of the night.

SARAH WILLIAMS

This night, the winter solstice, is the darkest night of the year.

We look for light at this time of year.

Among others, seek the lights of the night sky.

December 22

The secret of genius is to carry the spirit of youth into old age,
which means never losing your enthusiasm.

ALDOUS HUXLEY

One expects enthusiasm from the young—

which makes finding it in the old so alluring.

December 23

Sir, I am too old to learn.

WILLIAM SHAKESPEARE, *King Lear*

No, never!

Easier said than done.

It's the "old dog/new tricks" thing.

Not a trifling issue.

December 24

'Twas the night before Christmas and all thro' the house

Not a creature was stirring, not even a mouse . . .

CLEMENT CLARKE MOORE

It's part of the power of Christmas (or any "Big Day"): to anticipate . . .

All is still . . .

In preparation . . .

The day itself is almost surreal.

December 25

I will honor Christmas in my heart, and try to keep it all the year.

CHARLES DICKENS

These are the words of a chastened and repentant Ebenezer Scrooge in *A Christmas Carol*.

A fine literary example of a late-in-life conversion.

It can happen to anyone at all, at any time of life, with or without the help of Jacob Marley and his ghosts.

December 26

If you have a purpose in which you can believe, there's no end to the amount of things you can accomplish.

MARIAN ANDERSON

Today begins the season of Kwanzaa (through January 1st). Like HumanLight, a celebration of humanists on December 23rd, this is a modern (1966) celebration and honors African heritage in African American culture.

It is also a reminder to the world of the importance of celebrating cultures.

December 27

I've done a fair share of stupid things in my life, a couple of which should have put me in the grave. But here I am, typing away as if I had a brain.

CRAIG WILSON

"As if" is an important part of life.

Acting "as if" can often bring about the reality.

Fake it 'til you make it?

December 28

For the unlearned, old age is winter; for the learned it is the season of the harvest.

TALMUD

The holy book gives a choice: winter or harvest; a long, cold season or the reaping of blessings. A choice.

I believe "learned" here does not mean the educated, but the wise.

December 29

For any culture which is primarily concerned with meaning, the study of death—the only certainty that life holds for us—must be central, for an understanding of death is the key to liberation in life.

STANISLAV GROF

We have visited this idea now several times, in different forms.

It bears repeating because it has proven, over the centuries of human history, to be a difficult lesson to accept.

December 30

Still, still, still, One can hear the falling snow.

TRADITIONAL CAROL

And fortunate you are if you have indeed "heard the falling snow."

It seems important to take some time, now at the ending of the year, in snow or in sun, to pause in stillness and

Look ahead? Who knows?

Look back? All gone!

Just now.

December 31

Cheers to a new year
and another chance for us to get it right.

OPRAH WINFREY

Another chance!

Another chance!

Thank God almighty!

Another chance!

January

Ecology, Peace, and Mindfulness

January 1

The first law of ecology is that everything is related to everything else.

BARRY COMMONER

The "first" law.

"Everything."

We are all—things, people, nature, stuff, everything—in this together, related; we are "relatives" who need to get along with each other, who need each other.

When we really get this concept, everything begins to change.

Happy New Year.

January 2

Difference is the essence of humanity. Difference is an accident of birth and should therefore never be the source of hatred or conflict.

The answer to difference is to respect it. Therein lies a most fundamental principle of peace: respect for diversity.

JOHN HUME

Hume is a major architect of the Northern Ireland peace accord. He knows what he's talking about.

Fundamental principle of peace = respect for diversity

Consider.

January 3

*I prefer winter and fall. When you feel the bone structure of
the landscape—the loneliness of it—the dead feeling of winter.
Something waits beneath it, the whole story doesn't show.*

ANDREW WYETH

Artists use the words "palimpsest" and "layering" to
indicate the colors and forms underneath the colors and
forms.

Seek the deeper layers of the winter landscape—whatever
that may look like where you are.

January 4

*I hope to be remembered as someone who made the earth a little
more beautiful.*

JUSTICE WILLIAM O. DOUGLAS

There are so many ways to make the earth more beautiful.

Including your ways—go ahead and name a few of them.

Thank you.

January 5

There is no way to peace; peace is the way.

A. J. MUSTE

Peace is not merely a distant goal that we seek, but a means by which we arrive at that goal.

MARTIN LUTHER KING, JR.

Peace comes from within. Do not seek it without.

BUDDHA

If you wish to experience peace, provide peace for another.

THE 14TH DALAI LAMA

There seem to be millions of insightful quotes on peace—

. . . and still so much need for it.

January 6

Naturally we would prefer seven epiphanies a day and an earth not so apparently devoid of angels.

JIM HARRISON

But that's not what we got, is it?

What we've got is a beautiful world with way too much pain—including yours and mine.

Can the beautiful world lessen our pain?

January 7

Old age is the most unexpected of all things that happen to a man.

LEON TROTSKY

Logically, this seems unlikely to be an accurate statement. Yet, from observation and experience, we know that it is true.

Isn't the human capacity for denial amazing?

(Not for you or me, of course.)

January 8

*I never had come up with a really profound and strong ges-
ture—nothing like Julia Butterfly's. So I figured the best thing
I could do was live by my beliefs. That's probably the most profound thing that anybody can do.*

DARYL HANNAH

Don't want to live in a tree for two years, like Julia Butterfly did? Me neither.

So I'll live more wholeheartedly by my beliefs.

January 9

*Rituals have a surprising degree of influence over how people
experience what comes next. They often make life better . . .
and increase pleasure in everyday activities . . . simply by making you more mindful.*

U.C. BERKELEY WELLNESS LETTER

Become more conscious of the little (and not so little) rituals in your life. I bet there are more than you expect.

Think of beginning and ending each day, meals and times
of eating, patterns at work . . .

Maybe begin some new ones.

January 10

I want to make it clear, if there is ever a conflict [between environmental quality and economic growth], I will go for beauty, clean air, water, and landscape.

JIMMY CARTER

How important is it to let the world know—now and after you're gone—just what you believe, what you stand for?

If it is important, how will you do it?

I think it's not so easy.

January 11

In meditation we discover our inherent restlessness. Sometimes we get up and leave. Sometimes we sit there but our bodies wiggle and squirm and our minds go far away. This can be so uncomfortable that we feel it's impossible to stay. Yet this feeling can teach us not just about ourselves but also about what it is to be human . . .

PEMA CHÖDRÖN

Somehow we resist simply staying with whatever is happening for us at the moment.

Simply staying with our experience.

Be gentle with yourself—and of course, never forget your sense of humor!

Just stay.

January 12

The future is not something out there flowing toward us; it is hidden inside things . . .

GEORGE JOHNSON (REFERRING TO A HOPI BELIEF)

Framing your idea of the future in this way could be a big step toward living in the present moment.

No more future rushing at you, but simply "hidden inside" the things and moments of your present life.

January 13

We have to abandon the conceit that isolated personal actions are going to solve this crisis [climate change]. Our policies have to shift.

AL GORE

I'm so tempted to respond: "Yeah, Yeah, Yeah! Blah, Blah, Blah." To quote Eliza Doolittle, "Words, words, words! I'm so sick of words!" Of course we need new policies! Who doesn't know that?

But on the other hand . . . someone has to keep telling us. Until finally it begins to happen.

So in the end—after I calm down—thanks, Al.

January 14

If you want to make peace with your enemy, you have to work with your enemy. Then he becomes your partner.

NELSON MANDELA

If you want peace, you don't talk to your friends. You talk to your enemies.

DESMOND TUTU

You cannot shake hands with a clenched fist.

MAHATMA GANDHI

Here are three very powerful voices . . .

. . . added to an older one:

Love your enemies . . . do good to those who hate you.

LUKE 6:27

January 15

I like these cold, gray winter days. Days like these let you savor a bad mood.

BILL WATTERSON, *Calvin and Hobbes*

Can you picture Calvin confiding this to Hobbes?

But sometimes it's true: Just let me be in a bad mood!

January 16

Everything is created twice, first in the mind and then in reality.

ROBIN S. SHARMA

Me: "I could never imagine doing that!"

You: "Then you never will."

Me: "Oh."

January 17

If in our daily life we can smile, if we can be peaceful and happy, not only we, but everyone will profit from it. This is the most basic kind of peace work.

THICH NHAT HANH

Poetry is an act of peace. Peace goes into the making of a poet as flour goes into the making of bread.

PABLO NERUDA

The monk and the poet emphasize a basic tenet of peacemaking:

We can do peace work every day—and almost every minute of every day.

Consider the ways.

January 18

Your intellect may be confused, but your emotions will never lie to you.

ROGER EBERT

Think about this for a moment and you will understand what he means.

What you feel is what you feel.

Always—even if it's hard to name sometimes.

January 19

Mindfulness is often spoken of as the heart of Buddhist meditation. It's not about Buddhism, but about paying attention. That's what all meditation is, no matter what tradition or particular technique is used.

JON KABAT-ZINN

It goes back to what my first grade teacher told me (over and over!):

"David! Be still and pay attention!"

It's all about paying attention.

January 20

After all it is those who have a deep and real inner life who are best able to deal with the irritating details of outer life.

EVELYN UNDERHILL

It's the inner life that has the power—is in control of whatever appears on the outside, what we do and say, where we go, how we act.

Attention to the inner life: it's what you're doing here, no?

January 21

I like trees because they seem more resigned to the way they have to live than other things do.

WILLA CATHER

Do you like trees too? Do you find them resigned to the way they have to live?

Notice them today.

They do seem content, no?

January 22

Be happy in the moment, that's enough. Each moment is all we need, not more.

MOTHER TERESA

In this moment, there is plenty of time. In this moment, you are precisely as you should be. In this moment, there is infinite possibility.

VICTORIA MORAN

I think these statements need some time, to consider . . .

Maybe you get right away what they're saying.

Or, like me, do you need a little time?

January 23

The natural world is the larger sacred community to which we belong. To be alienated from this community is to become destitute in all that makes us human. To damage this community is to diminish our own existence.

THOMAS BERRY

If so, how will we become more intimate with the natural world?

Dig in the dirt?

Walk on the earth?

January 24

"Am I crazy? . . . I feel like it sometimes."

"Maybe . . . but don't worry about it. You need to be a little bit crazy. Crazy is the price you pay for having an imagination. It's your superpower. Tapping into the dream. It's a good thing, not a bad thing."

RUTH OZEKI, *A Tale for the Time Being*

Yes. We do need to be a little crazy. If nothing else, it helps us understand and interpret a world that is, in many ways, completely crazy.

And besides, it lets you "tap into the dream!"

Breathe in. Breathe out. Let go.

January 25

We are like butterflies who flutter for a day and think it is forever.

CARL SAGAN

After all, what is the span of a human life up against the span of the universe? It's all relative, and our lives are relatively short.

Let's make the most of our Butterfly Lives.

January 26

The most fundamental harm we can do ourselves is . . . not having the courage and respect to look at ourselves honestly and gently.

PEMA CHÖDRÖN

And yet self-awareness is often the most challenging, the most difficult, and seems to be the most painful thing we are called upon to do.

And if you do it "gently" the pain that is expected is often not there.

January 27

A child said, What is the grass? fetching it to me with full hands;
How could I answer the child?. . . I do not know what it is any more than he.

WALT WHITMAN

What we don't know! There is so much! Still!

But also there is mystery,

in both what we know and what we don't.

January 28

Here, with whitened hair, desires failing, strength ebbing out of him, with the sun gone down and with only the serenity and the calm warning of the evening star left to him, he drank to Life, to all it had been, to what it was, to what it would be.

SEAN O'CASEY, *Sunset and Evening Star*

There's both a profound sadness together with a deep joy in those words, written by the Irish playwright about himself.

So human!

January 29

True happiness, we are told, consists in getting out of one's self; but the point is not only to get out—you must stay out; and to stay out, you must have some absorbing errand.

HENRY JAMES, *Roderick Hudson*

An "absorbing errand"—what an excellent concept!

It made me consider: Do I have an "absorbing errand"?

Some might know theirs in an instant! For others, it will take a while.

In any case, a worthwhile endeavor.

January 30

Winter, a lingering season, is a time to gather golden moments, embark upon a sentimental journey, and enjoy every idle hour.

JOHN BOSWELL

This winter:

Either gather a golden moment;

Or start a sentimental journey;

Or enjoy an idle hour.

Or all three.

January 31

The Holy Land is everywhere.

NICHOLAS BLACK ELK

The visionary Oglala Lakota reminds us that all the land is holy, not just certain parts, including the land you rest upon just now.

Holy land? Why is it holy?

Keep its holiness in mind as you tread upon it.

February

Creativity, Emotions, and Dissent

February 1

February is merely as long as is needed to pass the time until March.

J. R. STOCKTON

In the Southern Hemisphere, these are the dog days of summer: hot and sultry. But in northern climes they can also be dog days—long and dark and gray—waiting for the light of spring . . .

Are you waiting? For something? For someone?

February 2

The soul should always stand ajar.

EMILY DICKINSON

What a compelling image: The soul standing ajar.

Always ready to admit whatever experience awaits, ecstatic or mundane, and all in between.

February 3

"Dissent is the highest form of patriotism" is often attributed to Thomas Jefferson, but there is no evidence that he said or wrote this. He did, however say:

The spirit of resistance to government is so valuable on certain occasions that I wish it to be always kept alive.

Authority seems to need an energy to oppose it.

To keep it honest.

To keep it true.

Without that dissent . . .

Problems.

February 4

Sentiment without action is the ruin of the soul.

EDWARD ABBEY

Seeking healthy ways to express your feelings—

Not a bad way to live your life, no?

February 5

Love winter when the plant says nothing.

THOMAS MERTON

Nothing.

Silence.

Stillness.

Winter's here.

February 6

He did each single thing as if he did nothing else.

CHARLES DICKENS, *Dombey and Son*

Seems as good a definition of mindfulness as any—from Victorian England.

You've no doubt done it in twenty-first-century USA.

Keep it up.

February 7

If I'd known I was gonna live this long [100 years], I'd have taken better care of myself.

EUBIE BLAKE

The great jazz musician and ragtime pianist offers us a fine bit of irony.

He died shortly after he said it.

February 8

We must not confuse dissent with disloyalty. When the loyal
opposition dies, I think the soul of America dies with it.

EDWARD R. MURROW

"Loyal opposition"—such a fine expression. Or is it an
oxymoron?

Can you oppose and still be loyal?

I hope so!

February 9

Emotions are contagious. We've all known it experientially.
You know after you have a really fun coffee with a friend, you
feel good. When you have a rude clerk in a store, you walk
away feeling bad.

DANIEL GOLEMAN

And we're all of us contagious.

We can give or get a feeling "germ" so easily.

Almost without knowing it.

Be aware.

February 10

*The Eskimo has fifty-two names for snow because it is import-
ant to them; there ought to be as many for love.*

MARGARET ATWOOD

Some words for love:

Care

Kindness

Benevolence

Do others come to mind?

February 11

The creative mind plays with the objects it loves.

CARL JUNG

"Playmate! Come out and play with me!"

"Who's that calling?

"Who?!"

February 12

Genius is the ability to renew one's emotions in daily experience.

PAUL CÉZANNE

Cezanne painted the same mountain, over and over.

Renewing his feelings about it on a daily basis.

You can tell by looking at his work.

February 13

Don't ask what the world needs. Ask what makes you come alive, and go do it. Because what the world needs is people who have come alive.

HOWARD THURMAN

So, what makes you "come alive"?

Consider it for a few moments.

Important question, right?

February 14

I know of only one duty, and that is to love.

ALBERT CAMUS

This is love: to fly toward a secret sky, to cause a hundred veils to fall each moment. First to let go of life. Finally to take a step without feet.

RUMI

A twentieth-century French author and philosopher and a thirteenth-century Persian mystic speak of love.

You, speaking of love?

Happy Valentine's Day.

February 15

Winter is the time of promise because there is so little to do—or because you can now and then permit yourself the luxury of thinking so.

STANLEY CRAWFORD

Pretend

sometime this winter

that you have nothing to do.

Then do it.

What would a time of doing nothing look like for you?

February 16

It's so easy for propaganda to work, and dissent to be mocked.

HAROLD PINTER

Mocking something good would seem to be one of the most evil acts.

Precisely because it's so easy to do—and to get support for it.

February 17

One does not discover new lands without consenting to lose sight of the shore for a very long time.

ANDRÉ GIDE

Out there on your own.

Alone.

Or are you on a journey of discovery?

Courage.

February 18

Creativity is allowing yourself to make mistakes.
Art is knowing which ones to keep.

SCOTT ADAMS

The *Dilbert* cartoonist is certainly creative.

I wonder how often what we're laughing at is the result of his recognizing a happy mistake?

He didn't miss it.

February 19

Anxiety is the handmaiden of creativity.

T. S. ELIOT

Negativity is the enemy of creativity.

DAVID LYNCH

A little anxiety may help to keep us fresh and aware.

A little negativity can grow into too much.

"Anxious and positive" seems to be the ideal creative balance.

February 20

Be kind whenever possible.
It is always possible.

THE 14TH DALAI LAMA

Simple.

Often difficult.

Always worth the effort.

February 21

Man, when you lose your laugh you lose your footing.

KEN KESEY, *One Flew Over the Cuckoo's Nest*

There may be nothing more important than an active sense of humor to get you through the tough times.

Cultivate your funny bone.

February 22

These years in silence and reflection made me stronger and reminded me that acceptance has to come from within and that this kind of truth gives me the power to conquer emotions I didn't even know existed.

RICKY MARTIN

Think about:

Your emotions you didn't know existed.

Do you think you "have" some?

So?

February 23

I love writing. I love the swirl and swing of words as they tangle with human emotions.

JAMES A. MICHENER

Picture this:

> Words
> Swirling and swinging away
> as they tangle with your love and fear and joy . . .

What a creative mess!

February 24

Whatever you can do, or dream you can do, begin it. Boldness has genius, power, and magic in it.

ANONYMOUS

You've probably heard these words before.

Frequently quoted and falsely attributed to Goethe, this popular quote has a complex history and is probably just several quotes combined.

But no wonder it has such appeal.

What a compelling idea!

February 25

Of course I'll hurt you. Of course you'll hurt me. Of course we will hurt each other. But this is the very condition of existence. To become spring, means accepting the risk of winter. To become presence, means accepting the risk of absence.

ANTOINE DE SAINT-EXUPÉRY

Isn't one of the most dangerous self-deceptions the assumption that everything is always supposed to come out right, that life is supposed to be trouble-free?

Hurt—yours and mine—is "the very condition of existence."

But fortunately, not the only one!

February 26

Freedom is hammered out on the anvil of discussion, dissent, and debate.

HUBERT HUMPHREY

And we go on hammering and hammering. From the right, from the left.

Seems to me dissent is based,

first of all,

on

listening.

February 27

Here in America we are descended in blood and spirit from revolutionists and rebels—men and women who dare to dissent from accepted doctrine. As their heirs, may we never confuse honest dissent from disloyal subversion.

DWIGHT D. EISENHOWER

Too often we forget our origins.

To our detriment.

Remember: "The British are coming! The British are coming!"

February 28

To keep the heart unwrinkled, to be hopeful, kindly, cheerful, reverent—that is to triumph over old age.

THOMAS BAILEY ALDRICH

This seems a thoughtfully selected list of characteristics:

Hopeful—kind—cheerful—reverent.

But I especially like the "unwrinkled heart."

February 29 (For Leap Years)

The poet Sylvia Plath offers this thought:

And by the way, everything in life is writable about if you have the outgoing guts to do it, and the imagination to improvise. The worst enemy to creativity is self-doubt.

Everything is "writable about."

You just need "outgoing guts"

and "imagination to improvise."

And kill that "self-doubt."

Thank you, Sylvia.

A Few Selected Resources

Gunaratana, B. H. *Mindfulness in Plain English*. Boston: Wisdom Publications, 2002.

A meditation manual on Vipassana meditation, a type of Buddhist meditation. Clear and insightful.

Hanh, Thich Nhat. *Peace Is Every Step: The Path of Mindfulness in Everyday Life*. New York: Bantam Books, 1992.

All of Thich Nhat Hanh's books are valuable. This one consists of short, accessible chapters.

Kabat-Zinn, Jon. *Mindfulness for Beginners: Reclaiming the Present Moment—and Your Life*. Boulder, CO: Sounds True, 2012.

Kabat-Zinn is credited with bringing mindfulness meditation into everyday medical practice. All his work is worth reading or listening to.

Langer, Ellen J. *Mindfulness: 25th Anniversary Edition*. Philadelphia: DaCapo Press, 2014.

Here is a psychological approach to mindfulness, not based on Eastern traditions, and with a great deal of insight into human interactions.

Mindful Schools: *www.mindfulschools.org*

This website is a rich resource for learning and teaching mindfulness, especially with and for adolescents and children.

Tolle, Eckhart. *The Power of Now: A Guide to Spiritual Enlightenment.* Novato, CA: New World Library, 1999.

A modern classic, Tolle's message is simple: living in the now is the truest path to happiness.

Williams, Mark and Danny Penman. *Mindfulness: An Eight-Week Plan for Finding Peace in a Frantic World.* New York: Rodale, 2011.

This work is for those who would prefer a workbook format. It takes you through an eight-week program to achieve mindfulness.

About the Author

David Kundtz, S.Th.D., psychothera-
pist, author, speaker, and erstwhile priest
lives in Kensington, California, a small
community near Berkeley. His doctoral
degree is in pastoral psychology. His
other books are:

Stopping: How to Be Still When You Have to Keep Going

Quiet Mind: One-Minute Mindfulness

Nothing's Wrong: A Man's Guide to Managing His Feelings

Ministry Among God's Queer Folk: LGBT Pastoral Care

Awakened Mind: One-Minute Wake Up Calls

Coming To: A Biomythography

His website is *www.stopping.com*. He welcomes comments
and ideas at *dk@stopping.com*.

To Our Readers